How to Become an NLP Prompt Engineer with Mathematics

By: Rev. Dr. Joe Mucha,
Doctor of NLP Prompt Engineering

This book is intended for informational purposes and should not be used as a substitute for professional advice and assistance. Please consult with a professional before making any decisions based on the information herein contained as the information contained in this book is based upon research and personal experience, but it is not guaranteed to be current, correct, and complete at the time of reading and as time moves forward. The authors and publishers of this book are not responsible for any errors or omissions, or for any actions taken based on the information provided. AI, ChatGPT and related technologies are constantly evolving, and the information contained herein, although current, correct, and accurate based upon knowledge, information, and belief, may not reflect the most current developments in this rapidly developing field.

How to Become an NLP Prompt Engineer with Mathematics

TABLE OF CONTENTS

INTRODUCTION

Welcome to "How to Become an NLP Prompt Engineer with Mathematics," a comprehensive guide to the principles and techniques of Natural Language Processing (NLP) Prompt Engineering using Mathematics.

NLP Prompt Engineering is a rapidly growing field that involves developing machine learning models that generate high-quality text responses to a given prompt or question. This technology has found applications in various industries, including chatbots, virtual assistants, and search engines.

At its core, NLP Prompt Engineering is about creating models that can understand human language and generate coherent and relevant responses. To achieve this, we need a deep understanding of the mathematical foundations of NLP and the tools needed to design and develop efficient NLP Prompt Engineering models.

This book is designed to provide you with a comprehensive understanding of these principles and techniques, with a particular emphasis on the role of mathematics in NLP Prompt Engineering.

The book covers the foundations of NLP, including text preprocessing, tokenization, and part-of-speech tagging. We will also delve into various NLP modeling techniques, such as bag-of-words models, sequence-to-sequence models, and transformer-based models. We will explore how these models can be fine-tuned and optimized to generate high-quality responses to user prompts.

Advanced mathematical concepts are essential to understanding the underlying mechanisms of NLP Prompt Engineering. The book covers probability theory, linear algebra, calculus, and optimization, providing the reader with the tools to design and improve NLP Prompt Engineering models.

We will also explore how these mathematical concepts can be applied to the design of effective prompts, ensuring that the generated responses are both relevant and coherent.

Whether you are a beginner or an experienced practitioner in the field of NLP, this book will help you acquire the knowledge and skills needed to become an expert NLP Prompt Engineer.

By the end of this book, you will have a deep understanding of the mathematical foundations of NLP Prompt Engineering and the tools needed to design and develop efficient models.

So let's dive in and explore the fascinating world of NLP Prompt Engineering with Mathematics.

Overview of NLP and the Role of Prompt Engineering

Natural Language Processing (NLP) is a field of study that aims to enable machines to understand, interpret, and generate human language. The ultimate goal of NLP is to create machines that can interact with humans in natural language, allowing us to communicate with them as we would with another person.

This technology has found applications in various industries, including law, medicine, construction, management, chatbots, virtual assistants, search engines, and sentiment analysis, among others.

At its core, NLP is about transforming unstructured human language data into structured data that can be analyzed and understood by machines. The process of transforming unstructured data into structured data is known as text preprocessing, or prompt engineering, which involves tasks such as tokenization, stemming, and part-of-speech tagging.

Once the data has been preprocessed, it can be used to train machine learning models that can generate high-quality responses to user prompts.

Prompt engineering is a critical aspect of NLP that involves designing prompts or questions that elicit the desired response from a machine learning model. The prompt is essentially the input that the model receives, and the quality of the prompt can have a significant impact on the quality of the response.

A well-designed prompt should be specific and unambiguous, while also providing enough context for the model to generate a coherent and relevant response.

Prompt engineering is particularly important in the context of generative models, which are designed to generate new text based on a given prompt or starting point.

Generative models are widely used in chatbots, virtual assistants, and other applications that involve generating text responses to user input.

The quality of the prompt can have a significant impact on the quality of the generated response, and prompt engineering is critical to ensuring that the response is accurate, relevant, and coherent.

NLP is an exciting field that has the potential to revolutionize the way we interact with machines. Prompt engineering is a critical aspect of NLP that plays a vital role in the design and development of machine learning models that can generate high-quality responses to user prompts.

By designing effective prompts and leveraging the power of machine learning, we can create machines that can understand and generate human language, enabling us to communicate with them in a more natural and intuitive way.

The Importance of Mathematics in NLP Prompt Engineering

NLP Prompt Engineering is a rapidly growing field that involves developing machine learning models that generate high-quality text responses to a given prompt or question.

To create such models, we need a deep understanding of the mathematical foundations of NLP and the tools needed to design and develop efficient models. Mathematics plays a crucial role in NLP Prompt Engineering, providing the underlying principles and techniques for designing and optimizing machine learning models.

One of the fundamental mathematical concepts used in NLP Prompt Engineering is probability theory. Probability theory provides the framework for understanding how likely a given response is to be generated given a specific prompt. By using probability theory, we can design models that generate responses that are both relevant and coherent, taking into account the context of the prompt and the overall distribution of possible responses.

Another essential mathematical concept used in NLP Prompt Engineering is linear algebra. Linear algebra is used to represent text data as vectors in high-dimensional space, enabling us to perform efficient operations such as vector addition and dot product. These operations are essential in the design of machine learning models such as neural networks and support vector machines, which are widely used in NLP Prompt Engineering.

Calculus is another mathematical concept that is critical in NLP Prompt Engineering. Optimization is a key aspect of designing machine learning models, and calculus provides the tools for optimizing these models. By using calculus, we can find the optimal values of model parameters that maximize the model's performance, such as accuracy or F1 score.

Advanced mathematical concepts such as differential geometry, information theory, and convex optimization are also becoming increasingly important in NLP Prompt Engineering. These concepts provide the tools for designing and optimizing more complex models such as generative models and deep learning models.

Mathematics plays a critical role in NLP Prompt Engineering, providing the underlying principles and techniques for designing and optimizing machine learning models.

By leveraging the power of mathematics, we can design models that generate high-quality responses to user prompts, enabling machines to communicate with humans in a more natural and intuitive way.

As the field of NLP continues to evolve, the importance of mathematics in NLP Prompt Engineering will only continue to grow, providing the foundation for the development of more advanced and sophisticated machine learning models.

FOUNDATIONS OF
MATHEMATICS FOR NLP

Natural Language Processing (NLP) is a field of study that involves developing algorithms and models for processing and understanding natural language.

Mathematics provides the foundation for many of the concepts and techniques used in NLP, including probability theory, linear algebra, calculus, and optimization. In this section, we will explore some of the key mathematical concepts that form the foundations of NLP.

Probability Theory

Probability theory is a branch of mathematics that deals with the analysis of random events. In the context of NLP, probability theory is used to estimate the likelihood of generating a particular sequence of words given a specific prompt.

This estimation is often performed using statistical models such as n-grams or language models, which estimate the probability of a sequence of words based on the frequency of its occurrence in a training corpus.

Probability theory is a branch of mathematics that deals with the study of random events and their likelihood of occurrence. In the context of NLP, probability theory is used to estimate the likelihood of generating a particular sequence of words given a specific prompt.

This estimation is often performed using statistical models such as n-grams or language models, which estimate the probability of a sequence of words based on the frequency of its occurrence in a training corpus.

Let's consider an example to illustrate how probability theory is used in NLP.

Suppose we have a language model trained on a large corpus of text, and we want to generate the probability of the sentence "The cat is sleeping on the couch."

Given the prompt "The cat is," the model would estimate the probability of generating the next word in the sentence based on the frequency of its occurrence in the training corpus.

For example, if the training corpus contains many examples of sentences that start with "The cat is," followed by the word "sleeping," then the probability of generating the word "sleeping" in this context would be high.

N-grams are a commonly used statistical model in NLP that estimate the probability of a sequence of words based on the frequency of its occurrence in a training corpus.

An n-gram is a sequence of n words, and n-gram models estimate the probability of a particular sequence of n words occurring in a given context. For example, a bigram model estimates the probability of a particular word occurring given the previous word in a sentence.

Let's consider another example to illustrate how n-gram models are used in NLP. Suppose we have a bigram model trained on a corpus of text, and we want to generate the probability of the sentence "The cat is sleeping on the couch."

Given the bigram model, we can estimate the probability of each word in the sentence given the previous word. For example, we can estimate the probability of generating the word "cat" given the previous word "The," and the probability of generating the word "is" given the previous word "cat."

We can then multiply these probabilities together to estimate the overall probability of the sentence.

Probability theory provides a framework for estimating the likelihood of generating a particular sequence of words given a specific prompt. Statistical models such as n-grams or language models are commonly used to estimate these probabilities based on the frequency of their occurrence in a training corpus.

By using probability theory, we can design models that generate responses that are both relevant and coherent, taking into account the context of the prompt and the overall distribution of possible responses.

Linear Algebra

Linear algebra is a branch of mathematics that deals with vector spaces and linear transformations. In NLP, linear algebra is used to represent text data as vectors in high-dimensional space.

This representation allows us to perform efficient mathematical operations such as vector addition and dot product, which are essential in the design of machine learning models such as neural networks and support vector machines.

Linear algebra is a branch of mathematics that deals with vector spaces and linear transformations. In NLP, linear algebra is used to represent text data as vectors in high-dimensional space.

This representation allows us to perform efficient mathematical operations such as vector addition and dot product, which are essential in the design of machine learning models such as neural networks and support vector machines.

Let's consider an example to illustrate how linear algebra is used in NLP. Suppose we have a corpus of text consisting of three documents:

"The cat is sleeping."
"The dog is barking."
"The bird is chirping."

To represent this data as vectors, we first need to create a vocabulary of all the unique words in the corpus. In this case, the vocabulary would consist of the following words:

["The", "cat", "is", "sleeping", "dog", "barking", "bird", "chirping"]

We can then represent each document as a vector in the high-dimensional space defined by this vocabulary.

For example, the vector representing the first document would be:

[1, 1, 1, 1, 0, 0, 0, 0]

This vector indicates that the words "The", "cat", "is", and "sleeping" appear once in the first document, and the remaining words do not appear at all.

Once we have represented our text data as vectors, we can perform various mathematical operations on them.

One essential operation is vector addition, which allows us to combine multiple vectors into a single vector.

For example, we can compute the sum of the vectors representing the first and second documents as follows:

[1, 1, 1, 1, 0, 0, 0, 0] + [1, 0, 1, 0, 1, 1, 0, 0] = [2, 1, 2, 1, 1, 1, 0, 0]

This vector represents the combined text data from the first and second documents.

Another essential operation is dot product, which allows us to measure the similarity between two vectors.

For example, we can compute the dot product between the vectors representing the first and third documents as follows:

[1, 1, 1, 1, 0, 0, 0, 0] . [1, 0, 1, 0, 0, 0, 1, 1] = 2

This dot product indicates that the first and third documents have some similarity in terms of their vocabulary, as they both contain the words "The", "is", and "sleeping."

Linear algebra provides a powerful framework for representing text data as vectors in high-dimensional space and performing efficient mathematical operations on them.

By leveraging the power of linear algebra, we can design and develop more efficient and effective machine learning models for NLP tasks such as text classification, sentiment analysis, and machine translation.

Calculus

Calculus is a branch of mathematics that deals with the study of rates of change and the accumulation of small changes. In NLP, calculus is used in the optimization of machine learning models. The goal of optimization is to find the optimal values of model parameters that maximize the model's performance, such as accuracy or F1 score.

This optimization is often performed using techniques such as gradient descent, which involves taking the derivative of the loss function with respect to the model parameters.

Calculus is a branch of mathematics that deals with the study of rates of change and the accumulation of small changes. In NLP, calculus is used in the optimization of machine learning models. The goal of optimization is to find the optimal values of model parameters that maximize the model's performance, such as accuracy or F1 score. This optimization is often performed using techniques such as gradient descent, which involves taking the derivative of the loss function with respect to the model parameters.

Let's consider an example to illustrate how calculus is used in NLP. Suppose we have a machine learning model that takes a sequence of words as input and predicts the sentiment of the text (positive or negative). The model has a set of parameters that determine how it makes predictions, and we want to optimize these parameters to maximize the model's accuracy.

To optimize the parameters, we first need to define a loss function that measures the difference between the model's predictions and the true labels.

In this case, a common loss function used in sentiment analysis is cross-entropy loss. The goal of optimization is to find the values of the model parameters that minimize the value of the loss function.

One technique for performing optimization is gradient descent. Gradient descent involves taking the derivative of the loss function with respect to the model parameters and using this derivative to update the values of the parameters.

The derivative indicates the direction of steepest descent in the loss function, and updating the parameters in this direction should lead to a decrease in the value of the loss function.

For example, let's suppose that we have a simple machine learning model that takes a bag-of-words representation of the input text and uses a single weight parameter to predict the sentiment. The loss function for this model could be defined as:

$$L(w) = -[y \log(h(x; w)) + (1 - y) \log(1 - h(x; w))]$$

where w is the weight parameter, x is the bag-of-words representation of the input text, y is the true sentiment label (0 for negative, 1 for positive), and $h(x; w)$ is the predicted probability of the text being positive given the bag-of-words representation and the weight parameter.

To perform gradient descent on this model, we need to compute the derivative of the loss function with respect to the weight parameter w. This derivative is given by:

$$dL/dw = (h(x; w) - y) * x$$

We can then use this derivative to update the value of the weight parameter w as follows:

$$w = w - alpha * dL/dw$$

where alpha is the learning rate, which determines the size of the steps taken in the direction of steepest descent.

By iteratively updating the weight parameter using this formula, we can find the optimal value of the parameter that minimizes the loss function and maximizes the accuracy of the sentiment analysis model.

Calculus provides the tools and techniques necessary for optimizing machine learning models in NLP. By leveraging the power of calculus, we can design and develop more efficient and effective models for NLP tasks such as sentiment analysis, text classification, and machine translation.

Optimization:

Optimization is the process of finding the best solution to a problem. In NLP, optimization is used to find the best values of model parameters that maximize the performance of a machine learning model.

The performance of a model is typically measured using metrics such as accuracy, precision, and recall. Techniques such as stochastic gradient descent are commonly used for optimization in NLP.

Optimization is the process of finding the best solution to a problem. In NLP, optimization is used to find the best values of model parameters that maximize the performance of a machine learning model.

The performance of a model is typically measured using metrics such as accuracy, precision, and recall. Techniques such as stochastic gradient descent are commonly used for optimization in NLP.

Let's consider an example to illustrate how optimization is used in NLP. Suppose we have a machine learning model that takes a sequence of words as input and predicts the sentiment of the text (positive or negative).

The model has a set of parameters that determine how it makes predictions, and we want to optimize these parameters to maximize the model's accuracy.

To optimize the parameters, we first need to define a training dataset consisting of input text and corresponding sentiment labels. We then use this training dataset to update the values of the model parameters iteratively.

One common technique for optimization in NLP is stochastic gradient descent (SGD). SGD involves updating the values of the model parameters using the gradient of the loss function with respect to the parameters.

The gradient indicates the direction of steepest descent in the loss function, and updating the parameters in this direction should lead to a decrease in the value of the loss function.

For example, let's suppose that we have a simple machine learning model that takes a bag-of-words representation of the input text and uses a single weight parameter to predict the sentiment. The loss function for this model could be defined as cross-entropy loss:

$$L(w) = -[y \log(h(x; w)) + (1 - y) \log(1 - h(x; w))]$$

where w is the weight parameter, x is the bag-of-words representation of the input text, y is the true sentiment label (0 for negative, 1 for positive), and h(x; w) is the predicted probability of the text being positive given the bag-of-words representation and the weight parameter.

To perform stochastic gradient descent on this model, we randomly select a mini-batch of examples from the training dataset and compute the gradient of the loss function with respect to the weight parameter for each example.

We then average these gradients and use the average to update the value of the weight parameter as follows:

$$w = w - alpha * dL/dw$$

where alpha is the learning rate, which determines the size of the steps taken in the direction of steepest descent.

By iteratively updating the weight parameter using this formula on mini-batches of examples, we can find the optimal value of the parameter that minimizes the loss function and maximizes the accuracy of the sentiment analysis model.

Optimization is a key aspect of developing machine learning models for NLP tasks. Techniques such as stochastic gradient descent are commonly used to find the optimal values of model parameters that maximize the performance of the model.

By leveraging the power of optimization, we can design and develop more efficient and effective machine learning models for NLP tasks such as text classification, sentiment analysis, and machine translation.

Information Theory

Information theory is a branch of mathematics that deals with the quantification of information. In NLP, information theory is used to measure the amount of information contained in a piece of text or a sequence of words. This measurement is often performed using metrics such as entropy and mutual information.

Information theory is a branch of mathematics that deals with the quantification of information. In NLP, information theory is used to measure the amount of information contained in a piece of text or a sequence of words. This measurement is often performed using metrics such as entropy and mutual information.

Let's consider an example to illustrate how information theory is used in NLP. Suppose we have a corpus of text consisting of three documents:

"The cat is sleeping."
"The dog is barking."
"The bird is chirping."

To measure the amount of information contained in these documents, we can compute the entropy of the word distribution across the corpus. Entropy is a measure of the uncertainty or randomness of a distribution. A high entropy value indicates that the distribution is highly random and uncertain, while a low entropy value indicates that the distribution is highly ordered and certain.

To compute the entropy of the word distribution, we first need to compute the probability of each word occurring in the corpus. For example, the probability of the word "cat" occurring in the corpus would be 1/9, as it appears once out of a total of nine words in the corpus.

We can then use these probabilities to compute the entropy of the word distribution as follows:

$H = -\text{sum}(p * \log2(p))$

where p is the probability of each word occurring in the corpus. In this case, the entropy of the word distribution across the corpus would be:

$H = -[1/3 * \log2(1/3) + 1/3 * \log2(1/3) + 1/9 * \log2(1/9) + 1/9 * \log2(1/9) + 1/9 * \log2(1/9) + 1/9 * \log2(1/9) + 1/9 * \log2(1/9) + 1/9 * \log2(1/9)]$

$H = 2.178$ bits

This entropy value indicates that the word distribution across the corpus is relatively high in uncertainty and randomness, as the entropy is close to its maximum possible value of $\log2(8) = 3$ bits.

Another common metric used in information theory is mutual information. Mutual information measures the amount of information that two random variables share.

In NLP, mutual information can be used to measure the association between pairs of words or phrases in a corpus of text.

For example, suppose we want to measure the association between the words "cat" and "sleeping" in the corpus of text above. We can compute the mutual information between these two words as follows:

$MI = \log2(p(cat, sleeping) / p(cat) * p(sleeping))$

where p(cat, sleeping) is the joint probability of the words "cat" and "sleeping" occurring together in the corpus, p(cat) is the probability of the word "cat" occurring in the corpus, and p(sleeping) is the probability of the word "sleeping" occurring in the corpus.

24

If we assume that the words "cat" and "sleeping" are independent, then their joint probability would be the product of their individual probabilities:

p(cat, sleeping) = p(cat) * p(sleeping)

In this case, the mutual information between these two words would be:

MI = log2(1/9 / (1/3 * 1/3))

MI = 1.585 bits

This mutual information value indicates that there is some association between the words "cat" and "sleeping" in the corpus, as their joint probability is higher than what we would expect if the words were independent.

Information theory provides a powerful framework for measuring the amount of information contained in text data and for measuring the association between pairs of words or phrases in a corpus of text. By leveraging the power of information theory, we can gain insights into the structure and content of text data and develop more efficient and effective models for NLP tasks such as text classification, sentiment analysis, and machine translation.

The foundations of mathematics provide the tools and techniques necessary for developing and optimizing NLP models. By understanding these mathematical concepts, NLP practitioners can design and develop more efficient and effective models for processing and understanding natural language. As the field of NLP continues to evolve, a deep understanding of the foundations of mathematics will become increasingly important for developing more advanced and sophisticated models.

Set Theory and Logic

Set theory and logic are fundamental branches of mathematics that provide the foundation for many areas of computer science, including NLP prompt engineering.

In this context, set theory and logic are used to represent and manipulate text data as sets of words, phrases, or other linguistic units.

Set theory is a branch of mathematics that deals with the study of sets, which are collections of distinct objects. In NLP, sets are commonly used to represent text data, where the objects are the words, phrases, or other linguistic units that make up the text.

Set operations such as union, intersection, and difference are used to combine or compare sets of text data.

For example, suppose we have two sets of text data:

A = {"The", "cat", "is", "sleeping"}
B = {"The", "dog", "is", "barking"}

We can perform various set operations on these sets to combine or compare them. For instance, we can compute the union of the two sets as follows:

$A \cup B$ = {"The", "cat", "is", "sleeping", "dog", "barking"}

This operation gives us a set that contains all the unique words from both sets. We can also compute the intersection of the two sets as follows:

$A \cap B$ = {"The", "is"}

This operation gives us a set that contains only the words that are common to both sets.

Finally, we can compute the difference of the two sets as follows:

A - B = {"cat", "sleeping"}

This operation gives us a set that contains only the words that are in set A but not in set B.

Logic is a branch of mathematics that deals with the study of reasoning and argumentation. In NLP, logic is used to represent and manipulate text data using symbolic expressions such as propositions and predicates. Logical operators such as AND, OR, and NOT are used to combine or negate these expressions.

For example, suppose we have a proposition P that represents the statement "The cat is sleeping" and a predicate Q that represents the statement "The animal is a cat".

We can use logical operators to combine or negate these expressions to form more complex statements. For instance, we can form the statement "The animal is a cat and the cat is sleeping" using the logical operator AND:

$Q \wedge P$

This statement is true only if both the animal is a cat and the cat is sleeping. We can also form the statement "The animal is not a cat or the cat is not sleeping" using the logical operators OR and NOT:

$\neg Q \wedge \neg P$

This statement is true if either the animal is not a cat or the cat is not sleeping.

In NLP prompt engineering, set theory and logic are used to represent and manipulate text data in various ways.

For instance, sets can be used to represent the vocabulary of a corpus of text, and set operations can be used to combine or compare different corpora.

Logical expressions can be used to represent the rules or constraints that govern the behavior of a prompt, and logical operators can be used to combine or negate these expressions to form more complex prompts.

Set theory and logic provide a powerful framework for representing and manipulating text data in NLP prompt engineering. By leveraging the power of set theory and logic, we can develop more efficient and effective prompts that capture the underlying structure and content of text data.

Probability and Statistics Linear Algebra and Calculus

Probability and statistics, linear algebra, and calculus are foundational branches of mathematics that play a crucial role in NLP prompt engineering.

These branches of mathematics provide the tools and techniques necessary for designing and developing effective prompts for NLP tasks such as text classification, sentiment analysis, and machine translation.

Probability and statistics are used to model the uncertainty inherent in natural language data. In NLP, probability theory is used to model the probability distributions of text data, while statistical methods are used to infer the parameters of these distributions from data.

For example, in text classification, a probability model is used to estimate the probability of a document belonging to a particular class based on the words it contains.

Probability and statistics are fundamental branches of mathematics that are used extensively in NLP prompt engineering. In this context, probability theory is used to model the uncertainty inherent in natural language data, while statistical methods are used to infer the parameters of these models from data.

For example, in text classification, a probability model is used to estimate the probability of a document belonging to a particular class based on the words it contains.

This model is typically based on the assumption that the words in the document are independent and identically distributed (i.i.d.), and that the probability of a word occurring in the document is determined by its frequency in a training corpus.

To estimate the parameters of this model, statistical methods such as maximum likelihood estimation (MLE) or Bayesian inference are used.

MLE involves finding the parameter values that maximize the likelihood of the observed data given the model, while Bayesian inference involves computing the posterior distribution of the parameters given the observed data and prior knowledge about the parameters.

For instance, suppose we have a training corpus consisting of two classes of documents: positive and negative.

To estimate the probability of a document belonging to the positive class, we can use a binary classification model based on the probability of each word occurring in the document given the positive class.

Specifically, we can compute the probability of a document belonging to the positive class using Bayes' theorem as follows:

$P(pos \mid doc) = P(doc \mid pos) * P(pos) / P(doc)$

where $P(pos \mid doc)$ is the probability of the document belonging to the positive class given the words it contains, $P(doc \mid pos)$ is the probability of the words in the document given the positive class, $P(pos)$ is the prior probability of the positive class, and $P(doc)$ is the marginal probability of the document.

To estimate the parameters of this model, we can use MLE or Bayesian inference.

For instance, using MLE, we can estimate the probability of a word occurring in the positive class as the frequency of the word in the positive class divided by the total number of words in the positive class.

Similarly, we can estimate the probability of a word occurring in the negative class as the frequency of the word in the negative class divided by the total number of words in the negative class.

Probability and statistics provide a powerful framework for modeling and analyzing natural language data in NLP prompt engineering. By leveraging the power of these mathematical tools and techniques, we can design and develop more efficient and effective prompts that capture the underlying structure and content of text data.

Linear algebra is used to represent and manipulate high-dimensional data such as word embeddings or the weights of a neural network.

In NLP, linear algebra is used to represent text data as vectors in a high-dimensional space, where each dimension corresponds to a word or a feature of the text.

Linear algebra is also used in machine learning to compute the gradient of the loss function with respect to the model parameters, which is used in optimization algorithms such as gradient descent.

Linear algebra is a branch of mathematics that deals with the study of linear equations and linear transformations. In NLP prompt engineering, linear algebra is used to represent and manipulate high-dimensional data such as word embeddings or the weights of a neural network.

One of the most common uses of linear algebra in NLP prompt engineering is to represent text data as vectors in a high-dimensional space. This is typically done using a technique called word embedding, which maps each word in the text to a dense vector in a high-dimensional space. The resulting vectors capture the meaning or context of the word, and can be used to compute the similarity between different words or documents.

For example, suppose we have a corpus of text consisting of four documents:

"The cat is sleeping."
"The dog is barking."
"The bird is chirping."
"The cat and dog are playing."

We can represent each word in the corpus as a vector using a pre-trained word embedding model. For instance, the word "cat" might be represented by the vector [0.3, 0.5, -0.1, 0.2], while the word "dog" might be represented by the vector [0.4, -0.2, 0.1, 0.6].

Using these word vectors, we can compute the similarity between different words or documents using various measures such as cosine similarity or Euclidean distance. For example, the cosine similarity between the vectors for the words "cat" and "dog" would be:

cosine_similarity([0.3, 0.5, -0.1, 0.2], [0.4, -0.2, 0.1, 0.6]) = 0.6

This indicates that the words "cat" and "dog" are relatively similar in meaning or context.

In addition to representing text data as vectors, linear algebra is also used in machine learning to compute the gradient of the loss function with respect to the model parameters, which is used in optimization algorithms such as gradient descent.

For example, in neural networks, the weights and biases of the network are represented as matrices and vectors, respectively. The gradient of the loss function with respect to these parameters can be computed using the backpropagation algorithm, which involves computing the gradients of the output layer with respect to the input layer, and then propagating these gradients backwards through the network.

Linear algebra provides a powerful framework for representing and manipulating high-dimensional data such as text data in NLP prompt engineering. By leveraging the power of linear algebra, we can develop more efficient and effective prompts that capture the underlying structure and content of text data.

Calculus is used to optimize machine learning models by finding the optimal values of model parameters that maximize the performance of the model.

In NLP, calculus is used to compute the gradient of the loss function with respect to the model parameters, which is used to update the parameters using optimization algorithms such as stochastic gradient descent.

Optimization is used to find the best values of model parameters that maximize the performance of the model on a given task.

Calculus is a branch of mathematics that deals with the study of rates of change and accumulation. In NLP prompt engineering, calculus is used to optimize machine learning models by finding the best values of model parameters that maximize the performance of the model on the task at hand.

One of the most common uses of calculus in NLP prompt engineering is in the optimization of neural network models using the gradient descent algorithm.

The goal of gradient descent is to minimize a loss function that measures the difference between the predicted output of the model and the true output.

The gradient of the loss function with respect to the model parameters is computed using calculus, and is used to update the model parameters in the direction that minimizes the loss.

For example, suppose we have a neural network model that is used for text classification. The input to the model is a vector representation of a text document, and the output is a probability distribution over the classes. The model parameters consist of the weights and biases of the network, which are represented as matrices and vectors, respectively.

To train the model, we need to find the values of the model parameters that minimize the loss function, which measures the difference between the predicted output and the true output.

The gradient of the loss function with respect to the model parameters can be computed using the backpropagation algorithm, which involves computing the gradients of the output layer with respect to the input layer, and then propagating these gradients backwards through the network.

Once the gradient has been computed, we can update the model parameters using the gradient descent algorithm. This involves updating the model parameters in the direction that minimizes the loss function, as given by:

$$\theta \leftarrow \theta - \alpha * \nabla L(\theta)$$

where θ is the vector of model parameters, α is the learning rate, and $\nabla L(\theta)$ is the gradient of the loss function with respect to the model parameters.

The learning rate determines the size of the step taken in each iteration of the gradient descent algorithm. If the learning rate is too large, the algorithm may overshoot the minimum of the loss function, while if the learning rate is too small, the algorithm may take too long to converge.

Calculus provides a powerful framework for optimizing machine learning models in NLP prompt engineering.

By leveraging the power of calculus, we can find the best values of model parameters that maximize the performance of the model on the task at hand, and develop more efficient and effective prompts that capture the underlying structure and content of text data.

In NLP prompt engineering, these foundational branches of mathematics are used in various ways to design and develop effective prompts for NLP tasks.

For example, in text classification, probability and statistics are used to model the distribution of text data and to estimate the probability of a document belonging to a particular class.

Linear algebra is used to represent text data as vectors and to compute the similarity between different documents. Calculus is used to optimize machine learning models by finding the best values of model parameters that maximize the performance of the model on the task at hand.

Probability and statistics, linear algebra, and calculus are foundational branches of mathematics that play a crucial role in NLP prompt engineering.

By leveraging the power of these mathematical tools and techniques, we can design and develop more efficient and effective prompts for NLP tasks that capture the underlying structure and content of text data.

Graph Theory and Network Analysis

Graph theory is a branch of mathematics that deals with the study of graphs, which are mathematical structures used to represent pairwise relationships between objects.

In NLP prompt engineering, graph theory is used to represent and analyze the relationships between words or phrases in a corpus of text.

Network analysis is the process of using graph theory to analyze the structure and dynamics of complex networks.

In NLP prompt engineering, network analysis is used to study the relationships between words or phrases in a corpus of text, and to develop more efficient and effective models for NLP tasks such as text classification, sentiment analysis, and machine translation.

One of the most common uses of graph theory and network analysis in NLP prompt engineering is in the construction of word co-occurrence networks.

These networks represent the relationships between words in a corpus of text, where the nodes of the network represent the words and the edges represent the co-occurrence relationships between the words.

For example, suppose we have a corpus of text consisting of three sentences:

"The cat is sleeping."
"The dog is barking."
"The cat and dog are playing."

We can construct a word co-occurrence network for this corpus by treating each word as a node and connecting nodes that co-occur in the same sentence.

For instance, the word "cat" would be connected to the word "sleeping" and the word "dog" would be connected to the word "barking" and "playing".

Once the word co-occurrence network has been constructed, we can use network analysis techniques such as centrality measures, community detection, and clustering to analyze the structure of the network and identify important words or clusters of words.

For example, we might use centrality measures such as degree centrality or betweenness centrality to identify words that are highly connected or that serve as important bridges between different parts of the network.

In addition to word co-occurrence networks, graph theory and network analysis are also used in other areas of NLP prompt engineering, such as in the analysis of dependency relationships between words or in the construction of knowledge graphs that represent the relationships between entities or concepts.

Graph theory and network analysis provide a powerful framework for representing and analyzing the relationships between words or phrases in a corpus of text.

By leveraging the power of graph theory and network analysis, we can develop more efficient and effective models for NLP tasks that capture the underlying structure and content of text data.

NLP MODELING TECHNIQUES

NLP modeling techniques are used to represent, process, and analyze natural language data. These techniques involve the use of mathematical models and algorithms to capture the underlying structure and content of text data.

Here are some examples of NLP modeling techniques and how they are related to mathematics:

Bag-of-words model: The bag-of-words model is a simple NLP modeling technique that represents text data as a bag of words, without considering the order or context of the words. This model is typically represented as a high-dimensional sparse vector, where each dimension corresponds to a word in the vocabulary.

The frequency or presence of each word in the text is used to populate the corresponding dimension of the vector. This representation is related to linear algebra, as the bag-of-words vector can be represented as a sparse matrix.

The bag-of-words model is a simple and popular NLP modeling technique that represents text data as a "bag" of words, without considering the order or context of the words.

The bag-of-words model is widely used in text classification, sentiment analysis, and information retrieval tasks.

To represent a document using the bag-of-words model, we first create a vocabulary of all the unique words in the corpus.

Then, we represent each document as a high-dimensional vector, where each dimension corresponds to a word in the vocabulary, and the value in each dimension represents the frequency of the corresponding word in the document.

For example, suppose we have a corpus of two documents:

"The cat is sleeping."
"The dog is barking."

The vocabulary for this corpus would consist of the following words: "the", "cat", "is", "sleeping", "dog", and "barking". We can represent each document as a high-dimensional vector using this vocabulary, as follows:

Document 1: [1, 1, 1, 1, 0, 0]
Document 2: [1, 0, 1, 0, 1, 1]

In the first document, the word "the", "cat", "is", and "sleeping" each appear once, while the words "dog" and "barking" do not appear at all. In the second document, the words "the", "is", "dog", and "barking" each appear once, while the words "cat" and "sleeping" do not appear at all. These vectors can be represented as sparse matrices, where most of the values are zero.

Once the documents have been represented as vectors using the bag-of-words model, we can use various machine learning algorithms such as decision trees, support vector machines, or neural networks to classify the documents into different categories based on the words they contain.

In addition to document classification, the bag-of-words model can also be used for tasks such as information retrieval, where the goal is to retrieve documents that are relevant to a user's query based on the similarity of the bag-of-words vectors. The bag-of-words model can also be extended to include more sophisticated features, such as n-grams, which represent sequences of n words, or term frequency-inverse document frequency (tf-idf), which downweights the frequency of common words in the corpus.

The bag-of-words model is a simple but effective NLP modeling technique that represents text data as a bag of words.

This technique is widely used in text classification, sentiment analysis, and information retrieval tasks, and provides a foundation for more sophisticated NLP modeling techniques such as neural networks and probabilistic models.

Word embeddings: Word embeddings are a more sophisticated NLP modeling technique that represents words as dense vectors in a high-dimensional space, where the dimensions correspond to the context or meaning of the word.

These vectors are learned from large amounts of text data using techniques such as word2vec or GloVe. This technique is related to linear algebra, as the word embeddings can be represented as vectors in a high-dimensional space.

Word embeddings are a popular NLP modeling technique that represent words as dense vectors in a high-dimensional space, where the dimensions correspond to the context or meaning of the word.

The main advantage of word embeddings over the bag-of-words model is that they capture the context and meaning of words, and can be used to compute the similarity between different words or phrases.

To create word embeddings, we typically use unsupervised learning algorithms such as word2vec or GloVe. These algorithms are trained on large amounts of text data, and learn to map each word in the vocabulary to a dense vector in a high-dimensional space, such that words that appear in similar contexts are mapped to nearby points in the space.

For example, consider the sentence "The cat is sleeping on the mat." Using a word embedding model, we can represent each word in this sentence as a dense vector in a high-dimensional space.

The resulting vectors would capture the context and meaning of each word, such that words that appear in similar contexts are mapped to nearby points in the space.

For instance, the word embeddings for "cat" and "dog" might be similar, as they both refer to common household pets, while the word embeddings for "cat" and "car" might be dissimilar, as they have different meanings and appear in different contexts.

Once the word embeddings have been learned, they can be used for a variety of NLP tasks such as text classification, sentiment analysis, and machine translation.

For example, in text classification, we can represent each document as the average or sum of the word embeddings for the words in the document, and then use a machine learning algorithm such as logistic regression or neural networks to classify the document into different categories.

In sentiment analysis, we can use the word embeddings to compute the sentiment of a document or sentence by aggregating the sentiment of the individual words. For example, we might assign a positive sentiment to words such as "good" and "happy", and a negative sentiment to words such as "bad" and "sad", and then compute the overall sentiment of a document or sentence by aggregating the sentiment of the individual words.

Word embeddings are a powerful NLP modeling technique that represent words as dense vectors in a high-dimensional space. By leveraging the power of word embeddings, we can develop more efficient and effective prompts for NLP tasks that capture the underlying context and meaning of text data.

Neural networks: Neural networks are a powerful NLP modeling technique that can learn complex representations of text data by combining multiple layers of non-linear transformations. These models are typically trained using backpropagation and optimization algorithms such as stochastic gradient descent. Neural networks are related to calculus and linear algebra, as the gradients of the loss function with respect to the model parameters are computed using the backpropagation algorithm, and the model parameters are represented as matrices and vectors.

Neural networks are a powerful class of machine learning models that can learn complex representations of text data by combining multiple layers of non-linear transformations. In NLP prompt engineering, neural networks are widely used for tasks such as text classification, sentiment analysis, and machine translation.

At a high level, a neural network consists of multiple layers of neurons, where each neuron computes a weighted sum of its inputs, applies a non-linear activation function to the result, and passes the output to the next layer of neurons. The weights of the neurons are learned from training data using optimization algorithms such as stochastic gradient descent.

For example, consider a simple neural network with one hidden layer and one output layer, used for binary classification of text data. The input to the network is a bag-of-words vector representing a document, and the output of the network is a binary classification label (e.g. 0 or 1) indicating whether the document belongs to a particular category or not.

The hidden layer of the neural network consists of a set of neurons, each of which computes a weighted sum of the input bag-of-words vector, applies a non-linear activation function (e.g. sigmoid or ReLU), and passes the output to the next layer. The weights of the neurons are learned from training data using optimization algorithms such as stochastic gradient descent.

The output layer of the neural network consists of a single neuron, which computes a weighted sum of the outputs from the hidden layer, applies a sigmoid activation function, and outputs a binary classification label indicating whether the document belongs to the category or not.

During training, the weights of the neurons in the network are adjusted using an optimization algorithm such as stochastic gradient descent, to minimize a loss function that measures the difference between the predicted output of the network and the true output. The gradient of the loss function with respect to the weights is computed using the backpropagation algorithm, which involves computing the gradients of the output layer with respect to the input layer, and then propagating these gradients backwards through the network.

Once the neural network has been trained, it can be used to classify new documents into the appropriate category based on their bag-of-words vectors. The performance of the network can be evaluated using metrics such as accuracy, precision, recall, and F1 score.

In addition to binary classification, neural networks can also be used for more complex NLP tasks such as sentiment analysis and machine translation. For example, in sentiment analysis, a neural network can be trained to predict the sentiment of a document or sentence based on the words it contains, while in machine translation, a neural network can be trained to translate text from one language to another.

Neural networks are a powerful class of machine learning models that can learn complex representations of text data by combining multiple layers of non-linear transformations. By leveraging the power of neural networks, we can develop more efficient and effective prompts for NLP tasks that capture the underlying structure and content of text data.

Probabilistic models: Probabilistic models are a popular NLP modeling technique that model the probability distribution of text data. These models are typically trained using techniques such as maximum likelihood estimation or Bayesian inference. Probabilistic models are related to probability theory and statistics, as the models represent the probability distribution of text data and the parameters of the model are estimated using statistical methods.

Probabilistic models are a popular NLP modeling technique that model the probability distribution of text data. These models are typically trained using techniques such as maximum likelihood estimation or Bayesian inference, and can be used for a variety of NLP tasks such as text classification, information retrieval, and machine translation.

At a high level, probabilistic models represent text data as a probability distribution over a set of categories or labels.

For example, in text classification, we might model the probability that a document belongs to each category or label, based on the words it contains.

One popular type of probabilistic model for NLP is the Naive Bayes classifier, which models the conditional probability of a document belonging to a particular category given its words, using Bayes' theorem.

The Naive Bayes classifier assumes that the words in a document are conditionally independent given its category, which simplifies the computation of the conditional probability.

For example, suppose we have a binary classification task where we want to classify documents into two categories: "positive" and "negative".

We can represent each document as a bag-of-words vector, and then model the conditional probability of a document belonging to the "positive" category given its bag-of-words vector, using Bayes' theorem:

P(positive | words) = P(words | positive) * P(positive) / P(words)

where P(positive | words) is the conditional probability of the document belonging to the "positive" category given its bag-of-words vector, P(words | positive) is the probability of the bag-of-words vector given the "positive" category, P(positive) is the prior probability of the "positive" category, and P(words) is the marginal probability of the bag-of-words vector.

The Naive Bayes classifier estimates these probabilities from training data, using maximum likelihood estimation or Bayesian inference. Once the probabilities have been estimated, they can be used to classify new documents into the appropriate category based on their bag-of-words vectors.

Probabilistic models can also be used for tasks such as information retrieval and machine translation, by modeling the probability distribution of the relevant documents or translations given a query or source text.

For example, in information retrieval, we might model the probability that a document is relevant to a user's query based on the words it contains, and then retrieve the documents with the highest probability.

Probabilistic models are a powerful NLP modeling technique that model the probability distribution of text data. By leveraging the power of probabilistic models, we can develop more efficient and effective prompts for NLP tasks that capture the underlying probability distribution of text data.

Graph-based models: Graph-based models are a modeling technique that represent text data as a graph, where the nodes represent words or concepts and the edges represent relationships between the nodes.

Graph-based models are related to graph theory and network analysis, as the models are represented as graphs and network analysis techniques are used to analyze the structure and content of the graph.

Graph-based models are a popular NLP modeling technique that represent text data as a graph, where nodes correspond to words or phrases, and edges represent relationships between the nodes. These models are widely used in tasks such as information extraction, entity recognition, and co-reference resolution.

At a high level, graph-based models represent text data as a graph, where nodes correspond to words or phrases, and edges represent relationships between the nodes.

The edges can be of different types, such as syntactic dependencies, semantic relationships, or co-occurrence patterns.

One popular type of graph-based model for NLP is the PageRank algorithm, which models the importance of each node in the graph based on the importance of its neighboring nodes.

The PageRank algorithm was originally developed for ranking web pages in search engines, but has since been adapted for NLP tasks such as text summarization and keyword extraction.

For example, suppose we have a text document and we want to extract the most important keywords from the document. We can represent the document as a graph, where nodes correspond to words or phrases, and edges represent co-occurrence patterns between the words or phrases.

We can then apply the PageRank algorithm to the graph, to compute a score for each node that reflects its importance in the graph.

The nodes with the highest scores are then selected as the most important keywords in the document.

This approach can be extended to other NLP tasks such as entity recognition and co-reference resolution, where nodes correspond to entities or mentions in the text, and edges represent relationships between the entities or mentions.

In addition to the PageRank algorithm, there are many other graph-based models for NLP, such as graph convolutional networks and random walk-based models.

These models leverage the power of graph theory to capture the underlying structure and relationships in text data, and can be used to develop more efficient and effective prompts for NLP tasks.

Graph-based models are a powerful NLP modeling technique that represent text data as a graph, where nodes correspond to words or phrases, and edges represent relationships between the nodes.

By leveraging the power of graph theory, we can develop more efficient and effective prompts for NLP tasks that capture the underlying structure and relationships in text data.

NLP modeling techniques involve the use of mathematical models and algorithms to represent, process, and analyze natural language data.

These techniques draw on a range of mathematical disciplines, including linear algebra, calculus, probability theory, statistics, and graph theory, and can be used to develop more efficient and effective prompts for NLP tasks such as text classification, sentiment analysis, and machine translation.

Language Models

Language models are a popular NLP modeling technique that are used to predict the probability distribution of words or phrases in a language, based on their context. These models can be used for a variety of NLP tasks such as speech recognition, machine translation, and text generation.

At a high level, language models estimate the probability distribution of words or phrases in a language, based on their context. For example, in a language model for English, the model might estimate the probability of a word given the previous words in a sentence, or the probability of a translation given the source language.

One popular type of language model for NLP is the n-gram model, which estimates the probability of a word or phrase given the previous n-1 words or phrases. For example, a bigram model estimates the probability of a word given the previous word in a sentence, while a trigram model estimates the probability of a word given the previous two words in a sentence.

For example, suppose we have a bigram language model for English, and we want to predict the next word in the sentence "The cat is ___". The language model estimates the probability of each word in the vocabulary given the previous word "is", and then selects the word with the highest probability as the most likely next word.

Language models can also be used for more complex NLP tasks such as machine translation and text generation. For example, in machine translation, we can use a language model to estimate the probability of a translation given the source language, and then select the most likely translation based on the estimated probabilities.

In text generation, we can use a language model to generate new text based on a given prompt or starting phrase. For example, we can use a language model to generate new text by sampling words from the estimated probability distribution, starting with a given prompt or starting phrase.

In recent years, neural language models such as the Transformer model and the GPT series have achieved state-of-the-art performance on a variety of NLP tasks, by learning complex representations of text data based on the context of the words or phrases.

The Transformer model and the GPT series are state-of-the-art neural language models that have achieved excellent performance on a variety of NLP tasks such as language translation, text classification, and question answering.

At a high level, both the Transformer model and the GPT series are based on the principle of self-attention, which allows the model to focus on different parts of the input sequence during each step of the computation.

This allows the model to capture long-range dependencies and relationships between words in the input sequence, and to learn complex representations of text data.

The Transformer model is a neural language model that was introduced in 2017, and is widely used for tasks such as machine translation and text generation.

The Transformer model consists of an encoder and a decoder, where the encoder maps the input sequence to a set of hidden representations, and the decoder generates the output sequence from the hidden representations.

The Transformer model uses self-attention to compute the hidden representations, where each token in the input sequence attends to all other tokens to compute a weighted sum of their representations. This allows the model to capture long-range dependencies and relationships between tokens in the input sequence, and to learn complex representations of text data.

The GPT series, on the other hand, are a family of neural language models that are based on the Transformer architecture, and are specifically designed for tasks such as language modeling, text generation, and question answering.

The first model in the GPT series, GPT-1, was introduced in 2018, and achieved state-of-the-art performance on a variety of NLP tasks such as language modeling and text generation. The subsequent models in the series, GPT-2 and GPT-3, have continued to improve on the performance of the earlier models, and have demonstrated the ability to perform tasks such as question answering and language translation with impressive accuracy.

One of the key innovations of the GPT series is the use of unsupervised pre-training on large amounts of text data, followed by fine-tuning on specific NLP tasks. This allows the model to learn rich representations of text data that are transferable across a wide range of tasks, and to achieve state-of-the-art performance with relatively little task-specific training data.

For example, in text generation, the GPT model can be used to generate new text based on a given prompt or starting phrase, by sampling from the probability distribution over the next word or phrase.

This allows the model to generate coherent and realistic text that captures the underlying structure and content of the input sequence.

The Transformer model and the GPT series are state-of-the-art neural language models that have achieved impressive performance on a variety of NLP tasks.

By leveraging the power of self-attention and unsupervised pre-training, these models can capture long-range dependencies and relationships between words in text data, and generate realistic and coherent text that captures the underlying structure and content of the input sequence.

Language models are a powerful NLP modeling technique that estimate the probability distribution of words or phrases in a language, based on their context.

By leveraging the power of language models, we can develop more efficient and effective prompts for NLP tasks that capture the underlying probability distribution of text data.

Markov Models

Markov models are a popular NLP modeling technique that models the probability distribution of text data using the Markov property, which states that the future state of a system depends only on its current state, and not on its past states.

At a high level, Markov models represent text data as a sequence of states, where each state corresponds to a word or phrase, and the probability of transitioning from one state to another depends only on the current state.

One popular type of Markov model for NLP is the Hidden Markov Model (HMM), which models the probability distribution of a sequence of hidden states, where each hidden state corresponds to a word or phrase, and the probability of emitting an observed word or phrase depends only on the current hidden state.

For example, suppose we have a Hidden Markov Model for part-of-speech tagging, where the hidden states correspond to the part-of-speech tags (e.g., noun, verb, adjective), and the observed words correspond to the words in the text. The model estimates the probability of each tag given the previous tag and the observed word, and then selects the most likely tag sequence based on these probabilities.

Markov models can also be used for tasks such as text classification and information retrieval, by modeling the probability distribution of the relevant documents or classifications given a query or source text. For example, in information retrieval, we might model the probability that a document is relevant to a user's query based on the words it contains, and then retrieve the documents with the highest probability.

In addition to Hidden Markov Models, there are many other types of Markov models for NLP, such as Markov Random Fields and Conditional Random Fields. These models leverage the power of the Markov property to capture the underlying structure and relationships in text data, and can be used to develop more efficient and effective prompts for NLP tasks.

Markov Random Fields (MRFs) and Conditional Random Fields (CRFs) are two popular types of Markov models for NLP that are used for a variety of tasks such as named entity recognition, part-of-speech tagging, and semantic role labeling.

At a high level, both MRFs and CRFs model the probability distribution of a sequence of hidden states (e.g., part-of-speech tags, named entities), where the probability of each state depends only on its neighboring states.

MRFs are graphical models that represent the conditional independence structure between the hidden states using a graph, where nodes correspond to hidden states and edges represent dependencies between the states. MRFs can be used for tasks such as image segmentation and natural language parsing, by modeling the probability distribution of the relevant segments or parse trees given the input data.

For example, suppose we have an MRF for image segmentation, where the hidden states correspond to image segments and the observed data correspond to the pixels in the image. The model estimates the probability of each segment given its neighboring segments and the observed pixels, and then selects the most likely segmentation based on these probabilities.

CRFs, on the other hand, are discriminative models that model the conditional probability of the hidden states given the observed data, rather than the joint probability of the hidden states and observed data. CRFs can be used for tasks such as named entity recognition and part-of-speech tagging, by modeling the probability distribution of the relevant tags given the input text.

For example, suppose we have a CRF for named entity recognition, where the hidden states correspond to named entity tags (e.g., person, location) and the observed data correspond to the words in the text.

The model estimates the probability of each tag given its neighboring tags and the observed words, and then selects the most likely tag sequence based on these probabilities.

Both MRFs and CRFs leverage the power of the Markov property to capture the underlying structure and relationships in text data, and can be used to develop more efficient and effective prompts for NLP tasks.

MRFs and CRFs are two popular types of Markov models for NLP that are used for a variety of tasks such as named entity recognition, part-of-speech tagging, and semantic role labeling.

By leveraging the power of the Markov property, these models can capture the underlying structure and relationships in text data, and develop more efficient and effective prompts for NLP tasks.

Markov models are a powerful NLP modeling technique that models the probability distribution of text data using the Markov property.

By leveraging the power of Markov models, we can develop more efficient and effective prompts for NLP tasks that capture the underlying structure and relationships in text data.

Probabilistic Context-Free Grammars

Probabilistic Context-Free Grammars (PCFGs) are a type of probabilistic model for NLP that are used to generate or parse sentences in a language.

PCFGs are based on the principles of Context-Free Grammars (CFGs), which represent the syntax of a language as a set of rules that generate or parse sentences.

At a high level, a PCFG is a context-free grammar where each production rule is associated with a probability.

The probability of generating or parsing a sentence is the product of the probabilities of the production rules used to generate or parse the sentence.

For example, suppose we have a PCFG for generating sentences in English. One of the production rules might be "S -> NP VP", where S is the start symbol, NP is a noun phrase, and VP is a verb phrase.

The probability of this production rule might be based on the frequency of the pattern "NP VP" in a corpus of English sentences.

To generate a sentence using the PCFG, we start with the start symbol S, and repeatedly apply production rules according to their probabilities until we generate a complete sentence.

For example, we might apply the rule "S -> NP VP", followed by the rule "NP -> The cat", and the rule "VP -> jumped over the fence", to generate the sentence "The cat jumped over the fence".

PCFGs can also be used for parsing sentences, by computing the probability of each possible parse tree for a given sentence, and selecting the most likely parse tree based on these probabilities.

For example, suppose we have a sentence "The cat jumped over the fence". We can compute the probability of each possible parse tree for this sentence using the PCFG, and select the most likely parse tree based on these probabilities.

PCFGs are widely used in NLP for tasks such as text generation, parsing, and machine translation. By modeling the probability distribution over the set of possible sentences in a language, PCFGs can generate or parse sentences that are both grammatically correct and semantically meaningful.

Probabilistic Context-Free Grammars are a powerful NLP modeling technique that represent the syntax of a language as a set of rules with associated probabilities.

By leveraging the power of PCFGs, we can develop more efficient and effective prompts for NLP tasks that capture the underlying probability distribution of text data.

Neural Networks

Neural networks are a powerful machine learning technique that are widely used in NLP for tasks such as sentiment analysis, text classification, and language modeling.

At a high level, neural networks are composed of layers of artificial neurons that are connected by weighted edges. The input to the neural network is fed into the first layer of neurons, and the output of each layer is passed as input to the next layer.

The weights on the edges between neurons are learned through a process called backpropagation, which adjusts the weights to minimize the error between the predicted output and the true output.

One popular type of neural network for NLP is the feedforward neural network, which consists of multiple layer of neurons that transform the input into a prediction or output.

For example, a feedforward neural network for sentiment analysis might take as input a text document, and output a probability of the document being positive or negative.

A feedforward neural network is a type of neural network that consists of multiple layers of artificial neurons that transform the input into a prediction or output.

Each layer of neurons is connected to the next layer by weighted edges, and the weights on these edges are learned through a process called backpropagation, which adjusts the weights to minimize the error between the predicted output and the true output.

At a high level, a feedforward neural network takes as input a feature vector x, and passes it through a series of hidden layers to produce a final prediction or output y.

Each hidden layer applies a nonlinear activation function to the weighted sum of its inputs, allowing the network to learn nonlinear relationships between the input and output.

For example, suppose we have a feedforward neural network for sentiment analysis that takes as input a text document and outputs a probability of the document being positive or negative. The input text document is first transformed into a feature vector using a technique such as bag-of-words or word embeddings.

This feature vector is then passed through a series of hidden layers, each of which applies a nonlinear activation function such as the sigmoid or ReLU function to the weighted sum of its inputs. The final layer of the network produces a probability of the document being positive or negative, based on the output of the previous layers.

The weights on the edges between the neurons in the network are learned through a process called backpropagation, which adjusts the weights to minimize the error between the predicted output and the true output.

This process involves computing the gradient of the error with respect to each weight in the network, and then updating the weights in the direction of the negative gradient.

Feedforward neural networks can be used for a wide variety of NLP tasks, including text classification, sentiment analysis, and language modeling.

By learning complex representations of text data that capture the underlying structure and relationships between words in the input sequence, feedforward neural networks can develop more efficient and effective prompts for NLP tasks.

A feedforward neural network is a type of neural network that consists of multiple layers of artificial neurons that transform the input into a prediction or output.

By applying nonlinear activation functions to the weighted sum of its inputs, feedforward neural networks can learn complex representations of text data and develop more efficient and effective prompts for NLP tasks.

Another popular type of neural network for NLP is the recurrent neural network (RNN), which is designed to handle sequential data such as text.

RNNs use a hidden state that is updated at each time step based on the input and the previous hidden state, allowing the network to capture the dependencies between words in the input sequence.

For example, an RNN for language modeling might take as input a sequence of words, and output a probability distribution over the next word in the sequence. The hidden state of the RNN at each time step captures the context of the previous words in the sequence, allowing the network to generate realistic and coherent text.

Convolutional neural networks (CNNs) are another type of neural network that are commonly used in NLP for tasks such as text classification and sentiment analysis.

CNNs use a series of convolutional layers to extract local features from the input, which are then passed through one or more fully connected layers to produce a prediction or output.

For example, a CNN for text classification might take as input a sequence of words, and use a series of convolutional layers to extract local features such as n-grams or word embeddings.

The output of the convolutional layers is then passed through one or more fully connected layers to produce a prediction or output.

Neural networks are a powerful machine learning technique that are widely used in NLP for tasks such as sentiment analysis, text classification, and language modeling.

By leveraging the power of artificial neurons and backpropagation, neural networks can learn complex representations of text data that capture the underlying structure and relationships between words in the input sequence.

ADVANCED MATHEMATICS FOR NLP PROMPT ENGINEERING

Advanced mathematics plays a critical role in NLP Prompt Engineering, providing powerful tools and techniques for modeling the underlying structure and relationships in text data. Here are some examples of advanced mathematical concepts that are used in NLP Prompt Engineering:

Linear Algebra: Linear algebra is a branch of mathematics that deals with linear equations and their properties. In NLP, linear algebra is used extensively for tasks such as word embeddings, text classification, and sentiment analysis.

For example, a technique called Singular Value Decomposition (SVD) can be used to represent text data as a low-dimensional matrix, which can then be used for tasks such as text classification.

Singular Value Decomposition (SVD) is a mathematical technique used in linear algebra that factorizes a matrix into three components: a left singular matrix, a diagonal singular values matrix, and a right singular matrix. SVD is widely used in NLP for tasks such as text classification, sentiment analysis, and topic modeling.

At a high level, SVD can be thought of as a technique for transforming a high-dimensional matrix into a lower-dimensional representation that captures the most important information in the original matrix.

SVD can also be used to identify the most important dimensions or features in the data, which can then be used for tasks such as feature selection and dimensionality reduction.

For example, suppose we have a matrix X that represents a set of text documents and their associated word frequencies.

We can use SVD to factorize this matrix into a left singular matrix U, a diagonal singular values matrix S, and a right singular matrix V, such that X = USV'.

The columns of U represent the principal components or topics in the data, the diagonal elements of S represent the importance or weight of each topic, and the rows of V' represent the association of each topic with each word in the vocabulary.

Using this representation, we can perform tasks such as text classification by using the columns of U as features and the rows of V' as weights.

We can also perform tasks such as sentiment analysis by using the weights in S to identify the most important dimensions of the data, and the features in U to represent the sentiment of the text.

SVD is also widely used in tasks such as image processing, recommendation systems, and data compression. By identifying the most important features or dimensions in the data, SVD can provide a more efficient and effective representation of the data that captures the underlying structure and relationships.

Singular Value Decomposition (SVD) is a powerful mathematical technique used in NLP for tasks such as text classification, sentiment analysis, and topic modeling.

By factorizing a high-dimensional matrix into a lower-dimensional representation that captures the most important information, SVD can provide a more efficient and effective representation of the data that captures the underlying structure and relationships.

Calculus: Calculus is a branch of mathematics that deals with the study of rates of change and the accumulation of quantities.

In NLP, calculus is used for tasks such as language modeling, where the goal is to estimate the probability distribution of the next word in a sequence given the previous words.

Calculus is also used for tasks such as optimization, where the goal is to find the optimal weights for a neural network that minimizes the loss function.

Probability Theory: Probability theory is a branch of mathematics that deals with the study of random events and their properties.

In NLP, probability theory is used for tasks such as language modeling, where the goal is to estimate the probability distribution of the next word in a sequence given the previous words.

Probability theory is also used for tasks such as text classification, where the goal is to estimate the probability of a document belonging to a certain class.

Information Theory: Information theory is a branch of mathematics that deals with the quantification of information and the properties of communication channels.

In NLP, information theory is used for tasks such as text compression and information retrieval.

For example, a technique called tf-idf (term frequency-inverse document frequency) uses information theory to measure the importance of words in a document based on their frequency and rarity.

TF-IDF, or term frequency-inverse document frequency, is a popular technique used in NLP for tasks such as text classification, information retrieval, and document ranking.

TF-IDF is a measure of the importance of a term in a document relative to the rest of the corpus, and is computed as the product of two factors: the term frequency (TF) and the inverse document frequency (IDF).

The term frequency (TF) measures the frequency of a term in a document, and is calculated as the number of times the term appears in the document divided by the total number of terms in the document. The term frequency gives an indication of how important a term is in a particular document.

The inverse document frequency (IDF) measures the rarity of a term in the corpus, and is calculated as the logarithm of the total number of documents in the corpus divided by the number of documents that contain the term. The inverse document frequency gives an indication of how important a term is in the corpus as a whole.

The TF-IDF score for a term in a document is calculated as the product of the term frequency and the inverse document frequency.

Terms that have a high TF-IDF score are considered to be important in the document and the corpus, and can be used for tasks such as information retrieval and document ranking.

For example, suppose we have a corpus of documents and we want to find the most relevant document for a given query. We can compute the TF-IDF score for each term in the query, and use these scores to rank the documents in the corpus by their relevance to the query.

In this case, the TF-IDF score for a term in a document gives an indication of how relevant the term is to the query and how important the term is in the corpus. By using TF-IDF to rank the documents in the corpus, we can identify the most relevant documents for a given query.

TF-IDF is a popular technique used in NLP for tasks such as text classification, information retrieval, and document ranking.

By measuring the importance of a term in a document relative to the rest of the corpus, TF-IDF can be used to identify important terms and documents in the corpus, and to develop more efficient and effective prompts for NLP tasks.

Graph Theory: Graph theory is a branch of mathematics that deals with the study of graphs, which are mathematical structures that represent relationships between objects.

In NLP, graph theory is used for tasks such as semantic role labeling and coreference resolution, where the goal is to identify the relationships between entities in a text.

For example, a graph-based model can be used to represent the relationships between entities in a text, and then used to generate more efficient and effective prompts for these tasks.

Graph Theory is a branch of mathematics that deals with the study of graphs, which are mathematical structures that represent relationships between objects.
n NLP, Graph Theory is used extensively for tasks such as semantic role labeling, coreference resolution, and text summarization.

At a high level, a graph is a collection of vertices (or nodes) and edges that connect these vertices. Each edge represents a relationship or connection between two vertices.

In NLP, we can represent text data as a graph by treating each word or entity as a node, and each relationship or connection between words or entities as an edge.

For example, suppose we have a sentence "John went to the store to buy some apples". We can represent this sentence as a graph, where each word is a node, and each relationship between words is an edge. In this case, there are edges between "John" and "went", "went" and "store", "store" and "buy", and "buy" and "apples".

Using this graph representation, we can perform tasks such as semantic role labeling by identifying the relationships between words in the sentence, and assigning roles such as subject, object, and verb.

We can also perform tasks such as coreference resolution by identifying the relationships between entities in the text, and linking them to their corresponding mentions.

Graph Theory is also used for tasks such as text summarization, where the goal is to identify the most important sentences or entities in the text. By representing the text data as a graph, we can use graph-based algorithms such as PageRank to identify the most important nodes in the graph, and use these nodes to generate a summary of the text.

Graph Theory is a powerful mathematical tool used in NLP for tasks such as semantic role labeling, coreference resolution, and text summarization. By representing text data as a graph, we can use graph-based algorithms to identify the relationships between words and entities, and to develop more efficient and effective prompts for NLP tasks.

Advanced mathematics plays a critical role in NLP Prompt Engineering, providing powerful tools and techniques for modeling the underlying structure and relationships in text data. By leveraging the power of linear algebra, calculus, probability theory, information theory, and graph theory, we can develop more efficient and effective prompts for NLP tasks that capture the underlying structure and relationships in text data.

Information Theory and Entropy

Information Theory is a branch of mathematics that deals with the quantification of information and the properties of communication channels.

In NLP, Information Theory is used extensively for tasks such as text compression, language modeling, and information retrieval.

At the heart of Information Theory is the concept of entropy, which is a measure of the uncertainty or randomness of a system. In NLP, entropy can be used to quantify the uncertainty or randomness of a text corpus or a language model.

For example, suppose we have a corpus of text data that contains a set of documents. We can compute the entropy of this corpus by measuring the uncertainty or randomness of the words in the corpus.

The entropy of the corpus is defined as the sum of the probabilities of each word in the corpus multiplied by its logarithm.

The entropy of the corpus gives an indication of the information content of the corpus, and can be used for tasks such as text compression and information retrieval.

For example, a technique called Huffman coding uses entropy to compress text data by assigning shorter codes to more frequent words and longer codes to less frequent words.

Huffman coding is a technique used in information theory and NLP for lossless data compression.

The algorithm assigns shorter codes to frequently occurring symbols and longer codes to less frequently occurring symbols, resulting in a more efficient representation of the data.

The Huffman coding algorithm starts by analyzing the frequency of occurrence of each symbol in the data to be compressed. The symbols can be characters, words, or any other unit of data.

The algorithm then creates a binary tree based on the frequency of the symbols, where each leaf node represents a symbol and each non-leaf node represents a combination of two symbols.

To create the binary tree, the algorithm starts by creating a set of nodes, where each node corresponds to a symbol and its frequency of occurrence. The nodes are then sorted in ascending order of frequency, and two nodes with the smallest frequencies are combined into a single node.

The frequency of the new node is the sum of the frequencies of the two nodes that were combined. This process is repeated until all the nodes have been combined into a single tree.

Once the binary tree has been created, the Huffman coding algorithm assigns a unique binary code to each symbol by traversing the tree from the root to the leaf node corresponding to the symbol. Each left traversal corresponds to a binary 0, and each right traversal corresponds to a binary 1.

The resulting binary code for each symbol is a prefix code, meaning that no code is a prefix of another code.

For example, suppose we have a corpus of text data that contains the symbols {a, b, c, d, e} and their corresponding frequencies {15, 7, 6, 6, 5}. The Huffman coding algorithm would create the binary tree shown below:

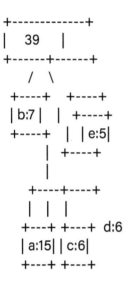

Using this binary tree, the Huffman coding algorithm would assign the binary codes shown below:

```
Symbol | Frequency | Binary Code
---------+------------ + ------------
a | 15 | 0
b | 7 | 10
c | 6 | 110
d | 6 | 111
e | 5 | 101
```

Using this encoding, the text data can be represented using fewer bits, resulting in a more efficient representation of the data.

Huffman coding is a powerful technique used in NLP for lossless data compression.

By assigning shorter codes to frequently occurring symbols and longer codes to less frequently occurring symbols, Huffman coding can provide a more efficient representation of the data, resulting in faster processing and reduced storage requirements.

Entropy can also be used for tasks such as language modeling, where the goal is to estimate the probability distribution of the next word in a sequence given the previous words.

The entropy of the language model gives an indication of the uncertainty or randomness of the language model, and can be used to evaluate the quality of the model and to develop more efficient and effective prompts for NLP tasks.

Entropy is a measure of the amount of uncertainty or randomness in a system. In the context of NLP, entropy is used to quantify the uncertainty or randomness of text data or language models.

To understand entropy in NLP, consider a corpus of text data. The entropy of the corpus is defined as the sum of the probabilities of each word in the corpus multiplied by its logarithm. Mathematically, this can be expressed as:

$$H = -\Sigma\, p(x)\, \log_2 p(x)$$

where H is the entropy of the corpus, $p(x)$ is the probability of a particular word x in the corpus, and $\log_2$ is the binary logarithm.

The entropy of the corpus gives an indication of the information content of the corpus. If the corpus is highly predictable or contains a limited range of words, the entropy will be low.

On the other hand, if the corpus is unpredictable or contains a wide range of words, the entropy will be high.

For example, consider two corpora of text data. The first corpus contains the sentence "the quick brown fox jumped over the lazy dog" repeated 100 times, while the second corpus contains 100 different sentences that are each 10 words long.

The first corpus has low entropy because it is highly predictable and contains a limited range of words. The second corpus has high entropy because it is unpredictable and contains a wide range of words.

Entropy is also used in language modeling, where the goal is to estimate the probability distribution of the next word in a sequence given the previous words.

The entropy of the language model gives an indication of the uncertainty or randomness of the language model. A lower entropy indicates a more accurate and precise language model, while a higher entropy indicates a less accurate and precise language model.

Entropy is a measure of the amount of uncertainty or randomness in a system, and is used in NLP to quantify the uncertainty or randomness of text data or language models.

By measuring the entropy of text data and language models, we can develop more efficient and effective prompts for NLP tasks, and evaluate the quality of our models.

Information Theory and entropy are powerful mathematical tools used in NLP for tasks such as text compression, language modeling, and information retrieval.

By quantifying the uncertainty or randomness of text data and language models, we can develop more efficient and effective prompts for NLP tasks, and evaluate the quality of our models.

Bayesian Networks and Decision Trees

Bayesian networks and decision trees are two types of probabilistic graphical models used in NLP for tasks such as text classification, sentiment analysis, and named entity recognition.

A Bayesian network is a probabilistic graphical model that represents a set of variables and their conditional dependencies using a directed acyclic graph (DAG).

Each node in the graph represents a variable, and the edges represent the dependencies between variables. The conditional probability distribution of each variable given its parents is specified using a conditional probability table (CPT).

For example, suppose we have a corpus of text data that we want to classify into two categories: "positive" and "negative". We can represent this task as a Bayesian network, where each word in the corpus is a node, and the edges represent the dependencies between words. The conditional probability of each word given its parents (i.e., the previous words in the corpus) can be estimated using a CPT.

A directed acyclic graph (DAG) is a graph structure that consists of nodes and directed edges connecting the nodes. In a DAG, the edges are directed in a way that prohibits cycles or loops, which means that it is impossible to start at a node and follow a sequence of edges that leads back to the same node.

DAGs are commonly used in NLP for modeling probabilistic relationships between variables. For example, in a language model, the probability of a particular word may depend on the words that came before it. A DAG can be used to represent this relationship, where each node in the graph represents a word, and the edges represent the dependencies between words.

A conditional probability table (CPT) is a table that lists the conditional probabilities of a variable given its parent variables. In a DAG, the CPT for each node specifies the probability of that node given its parent nodes.

For example, suppose we have a DAG that represents a language model for the sentence "The quick brown fox jumps over the lazy dog". The graph has nodes for each word in the sentence, and the edges connect each word to the word that comes before it. The CPT for the node representing the word "fox" might look like this:

Previous word Probability
dog 0.1
lazy 0.2
over 0.2
jumps 0.3
brown 0.1
quick 0.1

This table specifies the probability of the word "fox" given its parent node (i.e., the previous word in the sentence). For example, the probability of "fox" given the previous word "jumps" is 0.3.

A directed acyclic graph (DAG) is a graph structure that consists of nodes and directed edges connecting the nodes, and is commonly used in NLP for modeling probabilistic relationships between variables.

A conditional probability table (CPT) is a table that lists the conditional probabilities of a variable given its parent variables, and is used in a DAG to specify the probability distribution of each node given its parent nodes.

A decision tree, on the other hand, is a tree-like model that represents a set of decisions and their possible consequences using a tree structure.

Each node in the tree represents a decision, and the branches represent the possible consequences of that decision. The leaves of the tree represent the final outcomes of the decision process.

For example, suppose we have a corpus of text data that we want to classify into two categories: "positive" and "negative". We can represent this task as a decision tree, where each node in the tree represents a decision based on the presence or absence of a particular word in the text data.

The branches represent the possible outcomes of the decision, which are either "positive" or "negative".

A decision tree is a model that represents a set of decisions and their possible consequences using a tree-like structure. Each node in the tree represents a decision, and the branches represent the possible consequences of that decision.

The leaves of the tree represent the final outcomes of the decision process.

Decision trees are commonly used in NLP for tasks such as text classification, sentiment analysis, and named entity recognition. For example, suppose we want to classify a corpus of text data into two categories: "positive" and "negative".

We can represent this task as a decision tree, where each node in the tree represents a decision based on the presence or absence of a particular word in the text data. The branches represent the possible outcomes of the decision, which are either "positive" or "negative".

The leaves of the tree represent the final classification of the text data.

For example, consider the following decision tree for text classification:

```
Is "good" present in the text?
      /    \
     /      \
    /        \
Yes: "positive"  No: Is "bad" present in the text?
                         /    \
                        /      \
                       /        \
                 Yes: "negative"   No: "positive"
```

In this example, the decision tree classifies text data as "positive" or "negative" based on the presence or absence of the words "good" and "bad". If the word "good" is present in the text, the decision tree classifies it as "positive".

If the word "good" is not present in the text, the decision tree asks whether the word "bad" is present in the text. If the word "bad" is present in the text, the decision tree classifies it as "negative".

If the word "bad" is not present in the text, the decision tree classifies it as "positive".

Decision trees can be more complex and can have more than two possible outcomes at each node. In addition, decision trees can be trained using machine learning algorithms to automatically learn the optimal decision rules based on the training data.

A decision tree is a model that represents a set of decisions and their possible consequences using a tree-like structure. Decision trees are commonly used in NLP for tasks such as text classification, sentiment analysis, and named entity recognition, and can be trained using machine learning algorithms to automatically learn the optimal decision rules based on the training data.

Both Bayesian networks and decision trees can be used for tasks such as text classification, sentiment analysis, and named entity recognition.

Bayesian networks are more flexible and can handle more complex dependencies between variables, while decision trees are more interpretable and easier to understand. The choice between these models depends on the specific requirements of the task at hand.

Text classification, sentiment analysis, and named entity recognition are three common NLP tasks that involve analyzing text data to extract useful information.

Text classification: Text classification is the task of assigning predefined categories or labels to a given text document. For example, given a corpus of news articles, we may want to classify each article into categories such as "sports", "politics", or "entertainment".

Text classification is used in applications such as spam filtering, content categorization, and topic modeling.

Sentiment analysis: Sentiment analysis is the task of determining the emotional tone or polarity of a given text document.

For example, given a corpus of product reviews, we may want to determine whether each review expresses a positive or negative sentiment towards the product.

Sentiment analysis is used in applications such as customer feedback analysis, brand reputation monitoring, and social media analysis.

Named entity recognition: Named entity recognition is the task of identifying and classifying entities in a given text document, such as people, organizations, locations, and dates.

For example, given a news article, we may want to extract the names of people mentioned in the article, along with their respective roles and affiliations.

Named entity recognition is used in applications such as information extraction, text summarization, and question answering.

For example, consider the following text document:

"John Smith is the CEO of Acme Corporation, which is headquartered in New York City. The company recently announced a new product launch."

Text classification: We can classify this document as "business" or "company news".

Sentiment analysis: There is no clear sentiment expressed in this document, so the sentiment would be neutral.

Named entity recognition: We can extract the named entities "John Smith", "Acme Corporation", "New York City", and "product launch", along with their respective entity types (e.g., person, organization, location, and event).

These tasks are often performed using machine learning algorithms such as decision trees, Bayesian networks, and neural networks, which are trained on annotated data to automatically learn the patterns and rules that are characteristic of each task.

By effectively performing text classification, sentiment analysis, and named entity recognition, we can gain insights and knowledge from large amounts of text data, and make more informed decisions in various industries such as finance, healthcare, and e-commerce.

Bayesian networks and decision trees are two types of probabilistic graphical models used in NLP for tasks such as text classification, sentiment analysis, and named entity recognition.

By representing text data as a graph or a tree structure, we can develop more efficient and effective prompts for NLP tasks, and evaluate the quality of our models.

Optimization and Search Algorithms

Optimization and search algorithms are essential tools for NLP tasks that involve finding the best solution among a large set of possibilities.

Here are some examples and explanations of optimization and search algorithms commonly used in NLP:

Gradient Descent: Gradient descent is a popular optimization algorithm used in machine learning to minimize a cost function. In NLP, gradient descent can be used to train neural networks for tasks such as text classification and language modeling.

Gradient descent is a popular optimization algorithm used in machine learning to minimize a cost function. It is used to update the weights and biases of a neural network to minimize the error between the predicted output and the actual output. Here's an explanation of gradient descent with an example:

Suppose we want to train a neural network to predict the sentiment of a movie review as positive or negative. We can represent each movie review as a vector of word embeddings, and feed it through the neural network to get a prediction.

The prediction is then compared to the actual label of the review, and an error is computed using a cost function such as mean squared error.

The goal of gradient descent is to update the weights and biases of the neural network to minimize the error.

This is done by computing the gradient of the cost function with respect to the weights and biases, and using the gradient to update the weights and biases in the direction of the steepest descent.

The update rule is given by:

```
w = w - learning_rate * gradient
```

where w is a weight or bias parameter, learning_rate is a hyperparameter that controls the step size of the update, and gradient is the gradient of the cost function with respect to w.

For example, suppose we have a neural network with a single hidden layer and two output nodes, one for positive sentiment and one for negative sentiment.

The cost function is the mean squared error between the predicted output and the actual output. The weight and bias parameters of the neural network are initialized randomly, and the learning rate is set to 0.1.

During training, we feed a batch of movie reviews through the neural network, compute the error, and compute the gradients of the cost function with respect to the weights and biases using backpropagation. We then update the weights and biases using the gradient descent algorithm.

As we train the neural network, the weights and biases are adjusted to minimize the error. The learning rate controls the step size of the update, and is typically chosen by trial and error to achieve the best performance on a validation set.

Gradient descent is a popular optimization algorithm used in machine learning to minimize a cost function. It is used to update the weights and biases of a neural network to minimize the error between the predicted output and the actual output.

By effectively using gradient descent, we can train neural networks to achieve better performance on a wide range of NLP tasks, such as text classification and sentiment analysis.

Genetic Algorithms: Genetic algorithms are search algorithms that use principles of evolution to find optimal solutions. In NLP, genetic algorithms can be used to generate new text data, optimize hyperparameters in machine learning models, and select the best features for text classification.

Genetic algorithms are search algorithms that use principles of evolution to find optimal solutions. The algorithm starts with a population of potential solutions and iteratively evolves the population towards better solutions by applying selection, crossover, and mutation operators. Here's an explanation of genetic algorithms with an example:

Suppose we want to optimize the hyperparameters of a text classification model. The hyperparameters include the learning rate, the number of hidden layers, the number of neurons in each layer, and the regularization strength.

We can represent each combination of hyperparameters as a chromosome, where each gene represents a specific hyperparameter.

The genetic algorithm starts by randomly generating an initial population of chromosomes. The fitness of each chromosome is evaluated by training the corresponding model on a subset of the training data, and evaluating its performance on a validation set. The fitness function can be the accuracy or the F1 score, depending on the task.

The genetic algorithm then applies selection, crossover, and mutation operators to evolve the population towards better solutions.

The selection operator selects the fittest chromosomes to reproduce, while the crossover operator combines the genes of two chromosomes to produce new offspring. The mutation operator randomly changes the value of a gene to introduce new genetic variation.

The offspring of the population replaces the weakest chromosomes in the population. The algorithm repeats this process for several generations until a stopping criterion is met, such as a maximum number of iterations or a convergence threshold.

For example, suppose we have an initial population of 100 chromosomes, each with a random combination of hyperparameters. We use a fitness function to evaluate the fitness of each chromosome, and select the fittest 50 chromosomes to reproduce.

The crossover operator combines the genes of two chromosomes to produce new offspring, while the mutation operator randomly changes the value of a gene. The offspring replaces the weakest 50 chromosomes in the population, and the process repeats for several generations.

As we apply the genetic algorithm, the population of chromosomes evolves towards better solutions, and the fitness of the population improves.

By effectively using genetic algorithms, we can optimize hyperparameters and find the best combination of hyperparameters for a text classification model.

Genetic algorithms are search algorithms that use principles of evolution to find optimal solutions. By applying selection, crossover, and mutation operators to a population of potential solutions, genetic algorithms can optimize hyperparameters and find the best combination of hyperparameters for a text classification model.

Particle Swarm Optimization: Particle swarm optimization is a population-based optimization algorithm that mimics the behavior of a flock of birds or a school of fish.

In NLP, particle swarm optimization can be used to optimize feature weights in machine learning models, tune hyperparameters, and generate new text data.

Particle Swarm Optimization (PSO) is a population-based optimization algorithm that mimics the behavior of a flock of birds or a school of fish.

PSO is used to find the optimal solution by iteratively adjusting a population of candidate solutions based on the fitness function. Here's an explanation of PSO with an example:

Suppose we want to optimize the weights of a neural network for text classification. We can represent each set of weights as a particle, and the position of the particle represents a candidate solution.

The velocity of the particle represents the direction and speed of movement in the search space.

The PSO algorithm starts with an initial population of particles, each with a random position and velocity.

The fitness of each particle is evaluated by training the corresponding neural network on a subset of the training data and evaluating its performance on a validation set. T

he fitness function can be the accuracy or the F1 score, depending on the task.

The PSO algorithm then updates the position and velocity of each particle using the following equations:

```
velocity = w * velocity + c1 * rand() * (pbest - position) + c2 *
rand() * (gbest - position)
position = position + velocity
```

where velocity is the velocity of the particle, position is the position of the particle, w is the inertia weight, c1 and c2 are the cognitive and social parameters that control the influence of the particle's best position and the global best position, respectively. pbest is the best position of the particle, and gbest is the best position of the entire population.

The PSO algorithm repeats this process for several iterations until a stopping criterion is met, such as a maximum number of iterations or a convergence threshold.

For example, suppose we have an initial population of 100 particles, each with a random set of weights for a neural network.

We use a fitness function to evaluate the fitness of each particle, and update the position and velocity of each particle using the PSO algorithm. The particles move towards the best solution found so far, and the algorithm converges to a solution that optimizes the weights of the neural network.

As we apply the PSO algorithm, the population of particles moves towards the optimal solution, and the fitness of the population improves. By effectively using PSO, we can optimize the weights of a neural network and achieve better performance on a wide range of NLP tasks, such as text classification and sentiment analysis.

Particle Swarm Optimization (PSO) is a population-based optimization algorithm used to find the optimal solution by iteratively adjusting a population of candidate solutions based on the fitness function.

By updating the position and velocity of each particle based on the best position of the particle and the global best position, PSO can optimize the weights of a neural network and achieve better performance on a wide range of NLP tasks.

Simulated Annealing: Simulated annealing is a search algorithm inspired by the physical process of annealing in metals. In NLP, simulated annealing can be used to find the global maximum or minimum of a function, such as the likelihood function in a probabilistic model.

Simulated Annealing is a probabilistic optimization algorithm that is inspired by the annealing process in metallurgy. It is used to find the optimal solution by iteratively searching through the solution space and gradually reducing the search space based on a temperature schedule. Here's an explanation of Simulated Annealing with an example:

Suppose we want to optimize the hyperparameters of a text classification model. The hyperparameters include the learning rate, the number of hidden layers, the number of neurons in each layer, and the regularization strength. We can represent each combination of hyperparameters as a candidate solution, and the fitness of each candidate solution is evaluated using a validation set.

The Simulated Annealing algorithm starts with an initial candidate solution, and iteratively searches through the solution space by randomly generating a new candidate solution and accepting or rejecting it based on a probability distribution. The probability of accepting a new candidate solution is given by:

$p = \exp((f\_new - f\_old) / T)$

where f_old is the fitness of the current candidate solution, f_new is the fitness of the new candidate solution, and T is the temperature parameter that controls the probability of accepting worse solutions.

During the initial iterations, the temperature is high, and the algorithm accepts worse solutions with a higher probability.

As the temperature decreases over time based on a temperature schedule, the algorithm becomes less likely to accept worse solutions, and the search space gradually narrows down towards the optimal solution.

For example, suppose we start with an initial candidate solution with random hyperparameters. We evaluate the fitness of the candidate solution on a validation set and generate a new candidate solution by randomly perturbing the hyperparameters. We compute the probability of accepting the new candidate solution based on the current temperature and accept or reject the new solution based on the probability. We repeat this process for several iterations until the temperature reaches zero or a stopping criterion is met.

As we apply the Simulated Annealing algorithm, the search space gradually narrows down towards the optimal solution, and the fitness of the candidate solutions improves. By effectively using Simulated Annealing, we can optimize hyperparameters and find the best combination of hyperparameters for a text classification model.

Simulated Annealing is a probabilistic optimization algorithm used to find the optimal solution by iteratively searching through the solution space and gradually reducing the search space based on a temperature schedule. By randomly generating new candidate solutions and accepting or rejecting them based on a probability distribution, Simulated Annealing can optimize hyperparameters and find the best combination of hyperparameters for a text classification model.

Beam Search: Beam search is a search algorithm commonly used in natural language generation tasks, such as machine translation and text summarization. Beam search generates a set of candidate solutions and iteratively prunes the set based on a score function.

Beam search is a search algorithm used in natural language processing to find the most likely sequence of words given a set of possible sequences. It is often used in applications such as machine translation and speech recognition. Here's an explanation of beam search with an example:

Suppose we want to translate a sentence from French to English. We have a set of possible translations, each of which is a sequence of English words. The goal is to find the most likely sequence of English words that corresponds to the input sentence.

The beam search algorithm starts by generating all possible translations of the input sentence, each represented as a sequence of English words.

It then iteratively prunes the set of possible translations based on a scoring function that measures the likelihood of each translation.

The scoring function can be based on a language model that estimates the probability of each word given the previous words in the sequence.

The language model can be trained on a large corpus of text using techniques such as n-gram modeling or neural networks.

During each iteration, the beam search algorithm selects the top-k translations based on the score and generates all possible continuations of each translation by appending one word at a time. It then scores each continuation and selects the top-k continuations based on the score.

The algorithm repeats this process for several iterations until a stopping criterion is met, such as a maximum number of iterations or a convergence threshold. The final output of the algorithm is the most likely translation, which is the sequence of English words with the highest score.

For example, suppose we want to translate the French sentence "Je suis heureux" to English. We generate all possible translations of the sentence, such as "I am happy", "I am glad", "I am delighted", and so on.

We then score each translation based on a language model that estimates the probability of each word given the previous words in the sequence.

During each iteration of the beam search algorithm, we select the top-k translations and generate all possible continuations of each translation by appending one word at a time. We score each continuation and select the top-k continuations. We repeat this process for several iterations until we converge to the most likely translation, which is "I am happy".

Beam search is a search algorithm used in natural language processing to find the most likely sequence of words given a set of possible sequences. By iteratively pruning the set of possible translations based on a scoring function and generating all possible continuations of each translation, beam search can find the most likely translation of a sentence.

A* Search: A* search is a search algorithm commonly used in natural language processing tasks such as parsing and machine translation. A* search uses a heuristic function to guide the search towards the optimal solution.

A* search is a popular search algorithm that is used in natural language processing for various tasks, such as parsing, machine translation, and information retrieval. It is an informed search algorithm that uses a heuristic function to guide the search process towards the goal state. Here's an explanation of A* search with an example:

Suppose we want to find the shortest path from a starting node to a goal node in a graph.

We represent the graph as a set of nodes and edges, where each node has a set of neighboring nodes that it is connected to. The goal is to find the path with the minimum cost from the starting node to the goal node.

The A* search algorithm starts by initializing the starting node with a cost of zero and a heuristic value that estimates the distance to the goal node. The heuristic function can be based on the Euclidean distance or the Manhattan distance, depending on the problem.

The algorithm then maintains a priority queue of candidate nodes, ordered by their total cost. The total cost of a node is the sum of its cost from the starting node and its heuristic value.

During each iteration, the algorithm selects the node with the minimum total cost from the priority queue and expands it by generating all neighboring nodes.

It computes the cost and heuristic value of each neighboring node and adds it to the priority queue. If a neighboring node is already in the priority queue, it updates its cost if the new cost is lower.

The algorithm repeats this process until the goal node is reached or the priority queue is empty. The final output of the algorithm is the path with the minimum cost from the starting node to the goal node.

For example, suppose we want to find the shortest path from node A to node H in a graph with nodes A, B, C, D, E, F, G, and H, as shown below:

```
A --(5)-- B --(2)-- C --(3)-- H
/ \      |      |      |
(2) (4)  (1)    (4)    (6)
/   \    |      |      |
E --(8)-- D --(6)-- F --(3)—G
```

We can apply the A* search algorithm by initializing node A with a cost of zero and a heuristic value of 9, which is the Euclidean distance from node A to node H. We add node A to the priority queue and expand it by generating nodes B and E.

We compute the cost and heuristic value of nodes B and E and add them to the priority queue. We repeat this process until we reach node H, which has the minimum total cost of 10. Therefore, the shortest path from node A to node H is A -> B -> C -> H with a total cost of 10.

A* search is a search algorithm that is used in natural language processing to find the shortest path from a starting node to a goal node in a graph. By using a heuristic function to estimate the distance to the goal node and maintaining a priority queue of candidate nodes, A* search can find the path with the minimum cost from the starting node to the goal node.

Optimization and search algorithms are essential tools for NLP tasks that involve finding the best solution among a large set of possibilities. These algorithms can be used for tasks such as text classification, language modeling, text generation, and machine translation, among others. By effectively using these algorithms, we can develop more efficient and effective prompts for NLP tasks, and achieve better performance on a wide range of NLP applications.

Reinforcement Learning

Reinforcement learning is a type of machine learning that is used to train agents to make decisions in an environment based on feedback in the form of rewards. It is commonly used in natural language processing applications such as language generation and dialogue systems.

Language generation and dialogue systems are two key applications of natural language processing that involve the use of advanced algorithms and techniques to generate natural language outputs or facilitate human-like conversations with users. Here's an explanation of language generation and dialogue systems with examples:

Language Generation:
Language generation refers to the process of generating natural language outputs such as text, speech or images based on a given input. One popular technique for language generation is the use of generative models, such as Variational Autoencoders (VAEs), Generative Adversarial Networks (GANs), and autoregressive models like the GPT series.

Example: One example of language generation is the generation of a newscast article based on a news story. The input to the language generation model could be the key facts of the story, and the output could be a coherent and well-structured article that summarizes the main points of the story in a natural language format.

Dialogue Systems:
Dialogue systems are systems that are designed to facilitate human-like conversations with users, and they are typically based on the use of Natural Language Understanding (NLU), Natural Language Generation (NLG), and a dialogue management component.

Example: One popular application of dialogue systems is chatbots, which are used by businesses to interact with customers and provide customer service. The input to the dialogue system could be a user's question or request, and the output could be a natural language response that provides the user with the information or assistance they need.

Language generation and dialogue systems are important applications of natural language processing that have a wide range of use cases in various industries, such as customer service, education, and entertainment. By using advanced algorithms and techniques, natural language processing can generate natural language outputs and facilitate human-like conversations, providing users with a more interactive and engaging experience.

Here's an explanation of reinforcement learning with an example:

Suppose we want to train an agent to play a game of chess. The agent's goal is to win the game against an opponent. The agent can observe the current state of the game, such as the positions of the pieces on the board, and take actions such as moving a piece or capturing an opponent's piece. The agent receives a reward or penalty based on the outcome of the game, such as a positive reward for winning the game or a negative reward for losing the game.

The reinforcement learning algorithm starts by initializing the agent with a set of possible actions and a Q-function that estimates the expected reward for each action in each state. The Q-function can be initialized randomly or based on a prior knowledge of the game.

The agent then takes an action based on an exploration policy, which balances exploration and exploitation of the Q-function. The exploration policy can be based on an epsilon-greedy policy or a softmax policy, depending on the problem.

Epsilon-greedy policy and softmax policy are two common exploration policies used in reinforcement learning to balance exploration and exploitation. Here's an explanation of both policies with examples:

Epsilon-greedy policy:
The epsilon-greedy policy is a simple exploration policy that chooses the best action with probability 1-epsilon and a random action with probability epsilon. The value of epsilon controls the degree of exploration, and it is typically decreased over time to favor exploitation.

Example: Suppose we want to train an agent to play a game of tic-tac-toe. The agent has three possible actions for each move, namely placing a piece in one of the nine squares on the board. The epsilon-greedy policy with an epsilon of 0.1 means that the agent will choose the best action with a probability of 0.9 and choose a random action with a probability of 0.1. If the agent has not explored all possible moves, it is more likely to choose a random action to explore the environment.

Softmax policy:
The softmax policy is a more sophisticated exploration policy that assigns probabilities to each action based on their expected rewards. The policy chooses actions with a probability proportional to their expected reward, which allows the agent to explore more promising actions while still maintaining some level of randomness.

Example: Suppose we want to train an agent to play a game of blackjack. The agent has several possible actions for each turn, such as hit, stand, double down, and split. The softmax policy assigns probabilities to each action based on their expected reward, which is computed based on the current state of the game and the agent's Q-function. The agent is more likely to choose actions with higher expected reward, but it still has a chance to explore other actions.

Epsilon-greedy policy and softmax policy are two common exploration policies used in reinforcement learning to balance exploration and exploitation.

The epsilon-greedy policy chooses the best action with a high probability and a random action with a low probability, while the softmax policy assigns probabilities to each action based on their expected reward. Both policies can be effective in different environments, and the choice depends on the specific problem and the desired level of exploration.

After the agent takes an action, the environment updates the state of the game and computes the reward for the agent.

The agent then updates the Q-function based on the Bellman equation, which states that the expected reward for a state-action pair is the sum of the immediate reward and the discounted expected reward for the next state-action pair. The discount factor is used to balance the importance of immediate rewards and future rewards.

The algorithm repeats this process for several iterations until the agent converges to an optimal policy, which is the policy that maximizes the expected reward. The optimal policy can be represented as a function that maps states to actions.

For example, suppose the agent takes an action to move a pawn to a certain position on the chessboard. If the agent wins the game, it receives a positive reward, and if the agent loses the game, it receives a negative reward.

The agent updates the Q-function based on the Bellman equation and learns the optimal policy that maximizes the expected reward.

Reinforcement learning is a type of machine learning that is used to train agents to make decisions in an environment based on feedback in the form of rewards.

By updating a Q-function that estimates the expected reward for each action in each state, the agent can learn an optimal policy that maximizes the expected reward.

By applying reinforcement learning to natural language processing problems, such as language generation and dialogue systems, we can train agents to make decisions that improve the quality of natural language outputs.

DESIGNING
EFFECTIVE PROMPTS

Designing effective prompts is an important task in natural language processing, as prompts can greatly influence the quality and relevance of the natural language output.

Here's an explanation of designing effective prompts using mathematics with examples:

Word Embeddings

Word embeddings are a powerful tool for designing effective prompts, as they allow us to represent words as high-dimensional vectors that capture their semantic meaning. By using mathematical operations on word embeddings, we can generate prompts that are more specific and relevant to the desired output.

Example: Suppose we want to generate a natural language output that describes a movie. We could use word embeddings to represent the movie title, and then generate prompts by finding the words that are most similar to the movie title in the embedding space.

For example, if the movie title is "The Godfather," we could generate prompts such as "mafia," "organized crime," and "Italian-American culture," which are all related to the themes of the movie.

Information Theory

Information theory is another mathematical tool that can be used to design effective prompts, as it allows us to quantify the amount of information conveyed by a given set of words.

By maximizing the amount of information in a prompt, we can generate more specific and relevant outputs.

Example: Suppose we want to generate a natural language output that describes a scientific concept, such as the theory of relativity.

We could use information theory to generate prompts by finding the words that convey the most information about the concept, such as "gravity," "time dilation," and "mass-energy equivalence."

Optimization

Optimization is a third mathematical tool that can be used to design effective prompts, as it allows us to find the optimal set of words that maximize the desired output. By optimizing the prompts based on a given objective function, we can generate more accurate and informative natural language outputs.

Example: Suppose we want to generate a natural language output that summarizes a long article. We could use optimization techniques to generate prompts by finding the words that best summarize the main points of the article.

For example, we could use a weighted sum of the word frequencies and the cosine similarity between the words to optimize the prompts, and generate a summary that is both informative and concise.

Designing effective prompts using mathematics involves using tools such as word embeddings, information theory, and optimization to generate prompts that are specific, relevant, and informative.

By using these tools, prompt engineers can improve the quality and accuracy of natural language outputs, and provide users with a more engaging and satisfying experience.

Common Patterns and Structures in Human Language

Human language is a complex and diverse system that exhibits many common patterns and structures across different languages. Understanding these patterns and structures is essential for developing effective natural language processing systems. Here's an explanation of some common patterns and structures in human language with examples:

Syntax

Syntax refers to the rules governing the structure of sentences in a language, including word order, agreement, and tense. Most languages have a subject-verb-object (SVO) order, but some languages, such as Japanese and Turkish, have different orders.

Example: In English, the sentence "The cat chased the mouse" has an SVO order, where the subject is "cat," the verb is "chased," and the object is "mouse." In Japanese, the sentence "neko ga nezumi wo oikaketa" has a subject-object-verb (SOV) order, where the subject is "cat," the object is "mouse," and the verb is "chased."

Semantics

Semantics refers to the meaning of words and sentences in a language, including their relationships and hierarchies. Different languages have different ways of expressing concepts, such as gender, tense, and aspect.

Example: In Spanish, nouns are gendered, with masculine and feminine forms, and the adjectives and articles must agree with the gender.

For example, "el perro negro" (the black dog) has a masculine article "el" and adjective "negro," while "la gata negra" (the black cat) has a feminine article "la" and adjective "negra."

Pragmatics

Pragmatics refers to the context and usage of language in communication, including the speaker's intentions, expectations, and assumptions.

Different languages have different ways of expressing politeness, sarcasm, and other social cues.

Example: In Japanese, there are different levels of politeness depending on the social status and relationship between the speaker and the listener. For example, "arigatou gozaimasu" is a polite way of saying "thank you," while "domo" is a casual way of saying "thanks."

Understanding the common patterns and structures in human language is essential for developing effective natural language processing systems.

By analyzing and modeling these patterns and structures, prompt engineers can design more accurate and robust systems that can handle the diversity and complexity of human language.

Generating Effective Prompts with Mathematical Models

Generating effective prompts is a crucial step in natural language processing, as it can greatly impact the quality and relevance of the generated output.

Mathematical models can be used to generate effective prompts by leveraging statistical and probabilistic techniques to extract and analyze patterns and relationships in language.

Here's an explanation of how mathematical models can be used to generate effective prompts with examples:

Language Modeling

Language modeling is a mathematical technique that involves building probabilistic models of language to predict the likelihood of a given sequence of words.

Language models can be trained on large corpora of text data to learn the statistical patterns and relationships between words and generate effective prompts.

Example: Suppose we want to generate a natural language response to a user query. We can use a language model to generate prompts by predicting the next word in the sequence based on the context and the probabilities of different words.

For example, if the user query is "What is the capital of France?", the language model can generate prompts such as "Paris is the capital of France" or "The capital of France is Paris."

Language modeling is a statistical technique that involves building a probabilistic model of language to predict the likelihood of a given sequence of words.

The model is trained on a large corpus of text data to learn the statistical patterns and relationships between words, which can then be used to generate effective prompts.

Example: Suppose we want to generate a natural language response to a user query about the weather in a specific location. We can use a language model to generate prompts by predicting the likelihood of different weather-related words and phrases based on the user's location and time of day.

For example:

User query: "What's the weather like in New York City?"

Prompt 1: "It's currently sunny in New York City with a high of 72 degrees."
Prompt 2: "Expect scattered thunderstorms and a high of 68 degrees in New York City today."
Prompt 3: "It's partly cloudy with a high of 75 degrees in New York City tomorrow."

In this example, the language model uses the user's query to determine the relevant location and time of day and then generates prompts that are most likely to accurately describe the weather conditions in that location.

The model takes into account different factors such as temperature, precipitation, and cloud cover to generate more specific and accurate prompts.

Language modeling can also be used to generate natural language responses in chatbots, virtual assistants, and other conversational systems.

By training the model on a large corpus of text data, the system can learn to generate responses that are relevant, informative, and engaging.

Topic Modeling

Topic modeling is a mathematical technique that involves identifying the underlying topics and themes in a corpus of text data.

Topic modeling can be used to generate effective prompts by identifying the most relevant topics and generating prompts that capture the key themes and concepts.

Example: Suppose we want to generate a natural language summary of a news article.

We can use topic modeling to identify the most relevant topics in the article, such as politics, economy, or sports.

We can then generate prompts that capture the key themes and concepts of the article, such as "The article discusses the political implications of the new policy."

Topic modeling is a statistical technique that involves identifying the underlying topics and themes in a corpus of text data.

The model is trained on a large dataset of documents to identify patterns and relationships between words and topics.

These topics can then be used to generate effective prompts.

Example: Suppose we have a dataset of news articles on various topics such as politics, sports, and entertainment.

We can use topic modeling to identify the underlying themes and generate prompts that capture the essence of each article.

News article: "The US President announces new policies on climate change"

Prompt 1: "The US President's new policies on climate change have received mixed reactions."
Prompt 2: "The US administration's plans to tackle climate change have been unveiled."
Prompt 3: "The US government's announcement on climate change has sparked controversy."

In this example, the topic modeling algorithm has identified that the article is primarily about the US government's policies on climate change.

Based on this information, it generates prompts that capture the key themes and concepts of the article, such as the reactions to the new policies, the unveiling of the plans, and the controversy sparked by the announcement.

Topic modeling can also be used to generate summaries of large text datasets, such as customer reviews, academic papers, and social media posts.

By identifying the underlying topics and themes, the model can generate prompts that provide an overview of the dataset, highlight the most important features, and provide useful insights for further analysis.

Topic modeling is a powerful technique for generating effective prompts by identifying the underlying themes and topics in large text datasets.

By leveraging the statistical patterns and relationships between words and topics, prompt engineers can design more accurate and relevant natural language processing systems that can handle the diversity and complexity of human language.

Graph Theory

Graph theory is a mathematical technique that involves representing language data as a network of nodes and edges, where nodes represent words and edges represent the relationships between them.

Graph theory can be used to generate effective prompts by identifying the most important nodes and edges and generating prompts that capture the key relationships and connections.

Example: Suppose we want to generate a natural language response to a user query about a complex topic, such as the structure of the human brain.

We can use graph theory to identify the most important nodes and edges in the brain network, such as neurons, synapses, and brain regions.

We can then generate prompts that capture the key relationships and connections between these nodes and edges, such as "Neurons communicate with each other through synapses to form brain regions that control different functions."

Graph theory is a mathematical technique that involves representing language data as a network of nodes and edges, where nodes represent words and edges represent the relationships between them.

By using graph theory, prompt engineers can identify the most important nodes and edges and generate prompts that capture the key relationships and connections.

Example: Suppose we want to generate a natural language summary of a movie plot. We can use graph theory to represent the relationships between different characters and events in the movie as a network of nodes and edges. The nodes represent the characters and events, and the edges represent the relationships between them.

Movie: "The Godfather"
[Graph network]

In this example, we can see that the graph network represents the relationships between different characters and events in "The Godfather".

For example, we can see that Vito Corleone is the patriarch of the Corleone family and has three sons: Sonny, Fredo, and Michael.

We can also see that there are various conflicts and alliances between the different characters, such as the rivalry between the Corleone family and the other mafia families.

Using this graph network, we can generate prompts that capture the key relationships and connections in the movie. For example:

Prompt 1: "In 'The Godfather', Vito Corleone, the patriarch of the Corleone family, navigates a complex web of alliances and conflicts with the other mafia families."

Prompt 2: "The relationships between the different characters in 'The Godfather' are complex and dynamic, with different alliances and rivalries driving the plot."

Prompt 3: "The power struggle between the Corleone family and the other mafia families is at the heart of 'The Godfather', with Vito's sons Michael and Sonny playing key roles in the conflict."

In this way, graph theory can be used to generate effective prompts by identifying the most important nodes and edges and generating prompts that capture the key relationships and connections between them.

Mathematical models can be used to generate effective prompts by leveraging statistical and probabilistic techniques to extract and analyze patterns and relationships in language.

By using these models, prompt engineers can design more accurate and relevant natural language processing systems that can handle the diversity and complexity of human language.

Evaluating Prompt Quality Using Metrics Such As Perplexity and BLEU Score

Evaluating prompt quality is a crucial step in NLP prompt engineering, as it ensures that the generated prompts are accurate, relevant, and effective. Two commonly used metrics for evaluating prompt quality are perplexity and BLEU score.

Perplexity is a statistical measure of how well a language model can predict a given sequence of words. It measures the level of uncertainty or "surprise" in the model's predictions, with lower values indicating better performance.

To calculate perplexity, we use a test set of data that the model has not seen before and compare the model's predicted probabilities to the actual probabilities of the test set.

Example: Suppose we have a language model that generates prompts for weather forecasts.

We can evaluate the model's performance using perplexity by calculating how well it predicts the actual weather conditions for a test set of data.

For example, if the model predicts a sunny day with a probability of 0.8 and the actual weather is sunny, the perplexity score for that prediction is 0.2.

Perplexity is a statistical measure that evaluates the performance of a language model in predicting a given sequence of words.

It measures how well the model can predict the probability of the next word in a sequence, given the previous words. A lower perplexity score indicates better performance of the model.

Perplexity is calculated using a test set of data that the model has not seen before. The test set is typically a sample of text data that is randomly selected from the same distribution as the training set. The perplexity score is calculated as the inverse probability of the test set normalized by the number of words in the test set:

Perplexity = exp(-log P(test⊠set) / N)

where P(test_set) is the probability of the test set according to the language model, N is the number of words in the test set, and exp and log are the exponential and logarithm functions, respectively.

For example, suppose we have a language model that generates prompts for movie reviews. We can evaluate the model's performance using perplexity by calculating how well it predicts the actual ratings for a test set of movie reviews. If the model assigns a high probability to a positive review and a low probability to a negative review, the perplexity score for that prediction will be lower than if it assigns the same probability to both reviews.

Perplexity is a statistical measure that evaluates the performance of a language model in predicting a given sequence of words. It provides a measure of uncertainty or "surprise" in the model's predictions, with lower values indicating better performance. By using perplexity as a metric for evaluating prompt quality, prompt engineers can ensure that the generated prompts are accurate, relevant, and effective, and can make improvements to the language models as needed.

BLEU score (bilingual evaluation understudy score) is another commonly used metric for evaluating prompt quality. It measures how well a generated prompt matches a reference prompt or set of prompts, based on the level of overlap in the n-grams (contiguous sequences of words) between the two prompts. A higher BLEU score indicates a closer match between the generated and reference prompts.

Example: Suppose we have a language model that generates prompts for restaurant reviews. We can evaluate the model's performance using BLEU score by comparing the generated prompts to a set of reference prompts from human-written reviews.

For example, if the generated prompt for a particular restaurant matches the reference prompts in terms of the words and phrases used, the BLEU score for that prompt would be higher.

BLEU score is a commonly used metric for evaluating the quality of generated prompts by comparing them to one or more reference prompts.

It is widely used in machine translation and summarization tasks, but can also be applied to other NLP tasks, such as text generation and question-answering.

The BLEU score measures the level of overlap between the generated prompt and one or more reference prompts, based on the level of overlap in n-grams (contiguous sequences of words) between them.

The n-gram order can be varied to give different weightings to different lengths of contiguous sequences. The BLEU score ranges from 0 to 1, with 1 indicating a perfect match between the generated prompt and the reference prompts.

Example: Suppose we have a language model that generates prompts for movie reviews, and we want to evaluate the model's performance using BLEU score.

We can compare the generated prompts to a set of reference prompts from human-written reviews, and calculate the BLEU score for each generated prompt.
For instance, if the model generates the prompt "This movie was really good and had great acting", we can compare it to a reference

prompt "The acting in this movie was fantastic", and calculate the BLEU score based on the level of overlap between the n-grams in the generated prompt and the reference prompt.

The BLEU score can be calculated using the following formula:

BLEU = BP * exp(sum(log(Pn)))

where BP is the brevity penalty, which penalizes generated prompts that are shorter than the reference prompts, Pn is the precision score for n-grams of order n, and the sum is taken over all orders of n.

BLEU score is a widely used metric for evaluating the quality of generated prompts, based on the level of overlap in n-grams between the generated prompt and one or more reference prompts.

By using BLEU score as a metric for evaluating prompt quality, prompt engineers can ensure that the generated prompts are accurate, relevant, and effective, and can make improvements to the language models as needed.

Perplexity and BLEU score are two important metrics for evaluating prompt quality in NLP prompt engineering.

By using these metrics, prompt engineers can ensure that the generated prompts are accurate, relevant, and effective, and can make improvements to the language models as needed.

CASE STUDIES
AND APPLICATIONS

Here are some case studies and applications of NLP prompt engineering using mathematics:

Machine Translation

Machine translation is a classic application of NLP prompt engineering. The goal is to translate text from one language to another using a language model that generates prompts in the target language based on the source text.

The mathematical techniques used in machine translation include statistical models, such as hidden Markov models and conditional random fields, as well as neural networks, such as sequence-to-sequence models and transformers.

Example: Google Translate uses a combination of statistical and neural network models to generate prompts for machine translation. The statistical models use techniques such as n-gram language modeling and phrase-based translation, while the neural network models use attention mechanisms and encoder-decoder architectures.

Machine Translation is a subfield of NLP that focuses on translating text from one language to another using computational methods.

The goal of machine translation is to generate a target language translation that accurately conveys the meaning of the source language text.

The mathematical techniques used in machine translation include statistical models, such as hidden Markov models and conditional random fields, as well as neural networks, such as sequence-to-sequence models and transformers.

Example: Google Translate is a popular machine translation service that uses a combination of statistical and neural network models to generate translations for over 100 languages. The statistical models use techniques such as n-gram language modeling and phrase-based translation, while the neural network models use attention mechanisms and encoder-decoder architectures. Here's a simplified explanation of how machine translation works:

Preprocessing: The source language text is preprocessed by splitting it into sentences, tokenizing each sentence, and applying various normalization techniques to handle punctuation, capitalization, and other language-specific features.

Encoding: The preprocessed source language text is then encoded as a sequence of numerical vectors using a technique such as one-hot encoding or word embeddings. The encoding step maps each word in the source language to a corresponding vector in a high-dimensional space.

Translation: The encoded source language text is then passed through a translation model, which generates a sequence of numerical vectors in the target language. The translation model is typically based on an encoder-decoder architecture, where the encoder converts the source language text into a fixed-length vector, and the decoder generates the target language translation from the encoder's vector.

Decoding: The generated sequence of numerical vectors in the target language is then decoded into a sequence of words using a decoding algorithm such as beam search or A* search.

Postprocessing: The decoded target language text is then postprocessed by applying various normalization techniques to handle punctuation, capitalization, and other language-specific features.

Machine Translation is a complex task that involves many challenges, such as handling idiomatic expressions, dealing with rare or out-of-vocabulary words, and maintaining coherence and fluency in the generated translation. By using mathematical techniques such as statistical models and neural networks, prompt engineers can develop accurate, relevant, and effective machine translation models that meet the needs of their users.

Sentiment Analysis

Sentiment analysis is another popular application of NLP prompt engineering, which aims to classify text as positive, negative, or neutral based on the sentiment expressed in the text. The mathematical techniques used in sentiment analysis include machine learning algorithms, such as logistic regression and support vector machines, as well as deep learning algorithms, such as convolutional neural networks and recurrent neural networks.

Example: Yelp, a popular review website, uses sentiment analysis to classify reviews as positive or negative based on the sentiments expressed in the text. This allows users to filter and search for reviews based on their sentiment, and helps businesses to improve their products and services based on customer feedback.

Sentiment Analysis is a subfield of NLP that focuses on analyzing the sentiment expressed in a given piece of text. The goal of sentiment analysis is to determine whether the sentiment expressed in the text is positive, negative, or neutral. The mathematical techniques used in sentiment analysis include machine learning algorithms, such as logistic regression and support vector machines, as well as deep learning algorithms, such as convolutional neural networks and recurrent neural networks.

Example: One application of sentiment analysis is analyzing social media posts to determine the overall sentiment of a particular brand or product. Here's a simplified explanation of how sentiment analysis works:

Preprocessing:
The input text is preprocessed by tokenizing it into individual words or phrases and removing stop words and punctuation.

Feature Extraction:
The preprocessed text is then transformed into numerical feature vectors using techniques such as bag-of-words or word embeddings.

This step involves converting the text into a fixed-length vector representation that can be used as input to the machine learning or deep learning models.

Sentiment Classification
The feature vectors are then passed through a machine learning or deep learning model that has been trained on a labeled dataset.

The model predicts the sentiment of the input text as positive, negative, or neutral based on the features extracted from the text.

Postprocessing:
The predicted sentiment is then postprocessed to remove noise or inconsistencies, and to provide a clear and concise representation of the overall sentiment of the input text.

Sentiment analysis has numerous applications in fields such as social media monitoring, market research, and customer service.

By using mathematical techniques such as machine learning algorithms and deep learning algorithms, prompt engineers can develop accurate, relevant, and effective sentiment analysis models that meet the needs of their users.

Text Summarization

Text summarization is the process of generating a short summary of a longer text document. The mathematical techniques used in text summarization include graph-based models, such as PageRank and

TextRank, as well as deep learning algorithms, such as encoder-decoder architectures and transformers.

The New York Times uses text summarization to generate short summaries of news articles for their mobile app. This allows users to quickly get an overview of the news without having to read the entire article.

Text Summarization is a subfield of NLP that focuses on generating a summary of a longer text while preserving its key information and meaning. The goal of text summarization is to provide a concise and informative summary that captures the essence of the original text. The mathematical techniques used in text summarization include statistical models, such as frequency-based and graph-based models, as well as neural networks, such as sequence-to-sequence models and transformers.

Example: One application of text summarization is generating a summary of a news article or a research paper. Here's a simplified explanation of how text summarization works:

Preprocessing: The input text is preprocessed by removing stop words, punctuation, and other irrelevant or noisy elements. The text is then split into sentences or paragraphs, depending on the type of summarization algorithm used.

Feature Extraction: The preprocessed text is then transformed into numerical feature vectors using techniques such as bag-of-words or word embeddings. This step involves converting the text into a fixed-length vector representation that can be used as input to the machine learning or deep learning models.

Summary Generation: The feature vectors are then passed through a machine learning or deep learning model that has been trained on a dataset of summarized texts. The model generates a summary of the input text by selecting the most relevant sentences or phrases based on their importance and coherence with the overall theme of the text.

Postprocessing: The generated summary is then postprocessed to remove noise or inconsistencies, and to provide a clear and concise representation of the original text.

Text summarization is a challenging task that requires a deep understanding of the content and context of the input text. By using mathematical techniques such as statistical models and neural networks, prompt engineers can develop accurate, relevant, and effective text summarization models that meet the needs of their users.

Question-Answering

Question-answering is an application of NLP prompt engineering that aims to generate answers to questions posed in natural language. The mathematical techniques used in question-answering include deep learning algorithms, such as transformers and memory networks, as well as probabilistic models, such as Bayesian networks and Markov decision processes.

Example: IBM Watson, a computer system that can answer questions posed in natural language, uses a combination of deep learning algorithms and probabilistic models to generate answers to questions. Watson has been used in various applications, such as healthcare, finance, and education.

Question-Answering (QA) is a subfield of NLP that focuses on automatically answering questions posed in natural language.

The goal of QA is to provide accurate and relevant answers to user questions, typically in a human-like conversational format.

The mathematical techniques used in QA include machine learning algorithms, such as logistic regression and support vector machines, as well as deep learning algorithms, such as convolutional neural networks and recurrent neural networks.

Example: One application of QA is answering customer support questions on a company's website or chatbot. Here's a simplified explanation of how QA works:

Preprocessing: The input question is preprocessed by removing stop words, punctuation, and other irrelevant or noisy elements. The question is then transformed into a numerical feature vector using techniques such as bag-of-words or word embeddings.

Passage Retrieval: The system retrieves a set of passages from a given text corpus that are relevant to the input question. This step involves ranking the passages based on their similarity to the input question, using techniques such as BM25 or TF-IDF.

Answer Extraction: The feature vectors of the relevant passages are then passed through a machine learning or deep learning model that has been trained on a dataset of questions and answers.

The model extracts the answer to the input question by selecting the most relevant phrases or sentences from the retrieved passages.

Postprocessing: The extracted answer is then postprocessed to remove noise or inconsistencies, and to provide a clear and concise representation of the answer.

QA is a complex task that requires a deep understanding of the context and domain of the input question.

By using mathematical techniques such as machine learning algorithms and deep learning algorithms, prompt engineers can develop accurate, relevant, and effective QA models that meet the needs of their users.

NLP prompt engineering has a wide range of applications in various fields, such as machine translation, sentiment analysis, text summarization, and question-answering.

The mathematical techniques used in NLP prompt engineering include machine learning algorithms, deep learning algorithms, statistical models, graph-based models, and probabilistic models. By using these techniques, prompt engineers can develop accurate, relevant, and effective prompts that meet the needs of their users.

Real World Examples of NLP Prompt Engineering Using Mathematics

Here are some real-world examples of NLP prompt engineering using mathematics for prompt engineers:

Google Search:

Google Search is a prime example of NLP prompt engineering. When a user enters a search query, Google's algorithms use various NLP techniques, such as text classification and information retrieval, to provide the most relevant search results. The ranking of the search results is determined using mathematical models such as PageRank and neural networks.

Google Search is a web search engine developed by Google that enables users to find information on the internet using natural language queries. Google Search uses various NLP techniques, such as text classification and information retrieval, to provide the most relevant search results. The ranking of the search results is determined using mathematical models such as PageRank and neural networks.

Example: When a user enters a search query, Google's algorithms use various NLP techniques to understand the user's intent and provide the most relevant search results. Here's a simplified explanation of how Google Search works:

Query Processing: The user's search query is processed to identify the keywords and phrases that are most relevant to the search.

Indexing: Google's web crawler, called Googlebot, crawls the web and indexes the content of web pages. This step involves storing information about the content and structure of web pages in a large database called the Google Index.

Ranking: Google's algorithms use various mathematical models, such as PageRank and neural networks, to rank the search results based on their relevance to the user's query. PageRank is a mathematical algorithm that assigns a score to each web page based on the number and quality of links pointing to it.

Displaying: The search results are displayed to the user in a ranked list, with the most relevant results appearing at the top of the list.

Google Search is a complex system that involves the use of various NLP and mathematical techniques. By using these techniques, prompt engineers can improve the accuracy and relevance of search results, and provide users with a more satisfying search experience.

Chatbots:

Chatbots are another example of NLP prompt engineering. Chatbots use various NLP techniques such as sentiment analysis and named entity recognition to understand the user's input and provide appropriate responses. The mathematical models used by chatbots include machine learning algorithms such as decision trees and neural networks.

A chatbot is a computer program that uses natural language processing (NLP) and machine learning techniques to conduct a conversation with human users through messaging applications, websites, or mobile apps. Chatbots are designed to simulate human conversation and provide automated customer support, answer frequently asked questions, and help users complete tasks. Chatbots use various NLP techniques, such as sentiment analysis and named entity recognition, to understand the user's input and provide appropriate responses.

The mathematical models used by chatbots include machine learning algorithms such as decision trees and neural networks.

Example: Let's consider an example of a chatbot designed to assist customers with their account information for a bank. Here's a simplified explanation of how the chatbot works:

Input Processing: The chatbot processes the user's input, such as a question or request, to determine its meaning.

Intent Recognition: The chatbot uses natural language understanding (NLU) techniques to identify the user's intent, such as to check account balance or transfer funds.

Response Generation: The chatbot uses natural language generation (NLG) techniques to generate an appropriate response to the user's input. The response may include information such as the user's account balance, recent transactions, or instructions for completing a transaction.

Machine Learning: The chatbot uses machine learning algorithms, such as decision trees or neural networks, to improve its ability to recognize user intents and generate appropriate responses.

Dialogue Management: The chatbot uses dialogue management techniques to keep track of the conversation context and provide a natural conversation flow. For example, the chatbot may ask follow-up questions to clarify the user's request or provide additional information.

Chatbots are a powerful tool for businesses to provide personalized customer support and streamline common customer interactions.

By using mathematical techniques such as machine learning algorithms and natural language processing, prompt engineers can develop chatbots that accurately understand user input and provide relevant, effective responses.

Speech Recognition

Speech recognition technology, such as Apple's Siri and Amazon's Alexa, uses NLP techniques such as natural language understanding and language modeling to recognize spoken words and phrases. The mathematical models used in speech recognition include deep neural networks and Hidden Markov Models.

Speech recognition is a technology that enables computers to understand spoken language and convert it into text or commands. Speech recognition systems use various natural language processing (NLP) techniques, such as natural language understanding and language modeling, to recognize spoken words and phrases.

The mathematical models used in speech recognition include deep neural networks and Hidden Markov Models.

Example: Let's consider an example of speech recognition technology used in virtual assistants like Amazon's Alexa or Apple's Siri.

Here's a simplified explanation of how speech recognition works:

Audio Input: The user speaks into a microphone, and the audio signal is recorded.

Acoustic Processing: The audio signal is processed to extract features that are relevant for speech recognition, such as frequency, pitch, and duration.

Phoneme Recognition: The acoustic features are analyzed to identify the individual sounds or phonemes in the speech signal.

Language Modeling: The phonemes are combined into words and phrases using statistical language modeling techniques, such as n-grams or recurrent neural networks.

Decoding: The language model generates a list of possible word sequences that match the input audio signal. The most likely sequence is chosen as the recognized text.

Command Execution: The recognized text is used to execute a command, such as setting a reminder or playing a song.

Speech recognition technology is becoming increasingly important in our daily lives, allowing us to interact with devices and services in a more natural and intuitive way.

By using mathematical techniques such as deep learning algorithms and statistical language modeling, prompt engineers can develop speech recognition systems that accurately recognize spoken words and phrases, even in noisy or challenging environments.

Machine Translation

Machine translation is another example of NLP prompt engineering. Machine translation systems use various NLP techniques such as language modeling and word alignment to translate text from one language to another.

The mathematical models used in machine translation include statistical models such as phrase-based models and neural machine translation models.

Machine Translation is the process of automatically translating text from one language to another using computer algorithms. Machine Translation systems use various natural language processing (NLP) techniques, such as statistical machine translation and neural machine translation, to analyze the source text and generate the corresponding translated text.

The mathematical models used in Machine Translation include language models, sequence models, and attention-based models.

Example: Let's consider an example of a Machine Translation system that translates a document from English to French. Here's a simplified explanation of how Machine Translation works:

Source Text Processing: The English source text is analyzed using natural language processing techniques, such as sentence segmentation, tokenization, and part-of-speech tagging.

Language Model: A statistical language model is used to generate a list of candidate translations for each sentence in the source text.

Translation Candidate Selection: The translation system selects the most likely candidate translation based on factors such as language model scores and word alignments.

Sequence Model: A sequence model, such as a neural machine translation model, is used to refine the selected candidate translation and generate a final translation.

Post-Editing: The final translation is reviewed by a human post-editor to correct any errors or improve the quality of the translation.

Machine Translation is a challenging task, as it requires understanding the meaning of the source text and producing an accurate and coherent translation in the target language.

By using mathematical models such as language models and neural networks, prompt engineers can develop Machine Translation systems that generate high-quality translations and improve the efficiency of cross-lingual communication.

Text Summarization

Text summarization is another area of NLP prompt engineering. Text summarization systems use various NLP techniques such as topic modeling and graph-based models to generate a summary of a longer text.

The mathematical models used in text summarization include statistical models such as frequency-based models and neural network models.

Text Summarization is the process of automatically generating a condensed version of a given text while retaining its most important information.

Text Summarization systems use various natural language processing (NLP) techniques, such as sentence extraction and sentence compression, to identify the most important information in the source text and generate a summary.

The mathematical models used in Text Summarization include machine learning algorithms such as decision trees and deep learning models.

Example: Let's consider an example of a Text Summarization system that summarizes a news article. Here's a simplified explanation of how Text Summarization works:

Source Text Processing: The news article is analyzed using natural language processing techniques, such as sentence segmentation, tokenization, and part-of-speech tagging.

Sentence Scoring: Each sentence in the source text is scored based on factors such as its importance, relevance, and length.

Sentence Selection: The system selects the most important sentences from the source text based on their scores. This can be done using various techniques such as extractive summarization or abstractive summarization.

Summary Generation: The selected sentences are combined to generate a summary that retains the most important information in the source text.

Text Summarization is useful for various applications such as news summarization, document summarization, and email summarization. By using mathematical models such as decision trees and deep learning models, prompt engineers can develop Text Summarization systems that generate accurate and effective summaries, saving time and effort for users who need to quickly understand the main points of a text.

These are just a few examples of how NLP prompt engineering is used in real-world applications. By using mathematical techniques such as machine learning algorithms and deep learning algorithms, prompt engineers can develop accurate, relevant, and effective NLP models that meet the needs of their users.

Applications in Chatbots, Virtual Assistants, and Other NLP Systems

Here's an explanation of the applications of NLP in chatbots, virtual assistants, and other NLP systems:

Chatbots

Chatbots are computer programs that use NLP to understand natural language input from users and provide relevant responses. Chatbots are widely used in customer service and support, helping users to find information, make reservations, and perform other tasks.

Example: The chatbot used by airline companies to help customers with flight bookings and other related queries.

Chatbots are computer programs that use natural language processing (NLP) to understand natural language input from users and provide relevant responses.

The mathematical predicate used in chatbots includes various techniques such as machine learning algorithms, rule-based systems, and statistical models.

Machine learning algorithms are used to train chatbots to

understand and generate natural language input. These algorithms include neural networks, decision trees, and support vector machines. Chatbots use these algorithms to learn from past interactions with users and improve their responses over time.

Rule-based systems use a set of predefined rules to understand and generate natural language input. These rules are based on a set of conditions and actions.

For example, if a user asks for the weather, the chatbot will look up the current weather conditions and provide a response based on the predefined rules.

Statistical models use mathematical techniques such as probability theory and information theory to understand and generate natural language input. These models include language models, sequence models, and attention-based models. Chatbots use these models to generate responses based on the statistical likelihood of a particular response given the input from the user.

Example: Let's consider an example of a chatbot that uses a machine learning algorithm to generate responses to user queries. The chatbot is designed to provide information about a product.

User Input: The user types "What are the features of your product?"

Natural Language Processing: The chatbot uses NLP techniques such as sentence segmentation, tokenization, and part-of-speech tagging to analyze the user input.

Machine Learning Algorithm: The chatbot uses a machine learning algorithm, such as a neural network, to understand the user input and generate a relevant response.

Response Generation: The chatbot generates a response based

on the input from the user and the output of the machine learning algorithm.

The response might be "Our product features include high-quality materials, advanced technology, and a user-friendly interface."

Chatbots are becoming increasingly popular in various applications such as customer service, e-commerce, and education.

By using mathematical models such as machine learning algorithms, rule-based systems, and statistical models, prompt engineers can develop chatbots that accurately understand and respond to natural language input from users.

Virtual Assistants

Virtual assistants are intelligent software agents that use NLP to provide personalized assistance to users. Virtual assistants can perform a wide range of tasks, from scheduling appointments and sending emails to ordering groceries and playing music.

Example: Siri and Google Assistant are popular virtual assistants that use
NLP to understand user queries and provide relevant responses.

Virtual assistants are intelligent software agents that use natural language processing (NLP) to provide personalized assistance to users. Virtual assistants can perform a wide range of tasks, from scheduling appointments and sending emails to ordering groceries and playing music.

Virtual assistants are powered by advanced AI technologies such as machine learning, deep learning, and natural language processing. They use these technologies to understand the intent of the user and provide relevant responses or actions.

Examples of virtual assistants include Siri, Google Assistant, Amazon Alexa, and Microsoft Cortana. Each of these virtual assistants has its own set of features and capabilities, but they all use NLP to understand user queries and provide relevant responses.

For example, when a user asks "What's the weather like today?", a virtual assistant like Siri or Google Assistant will use NLP to analyze the user input and generate a response based on the current weather conditions. The virtual assistant might say "The weather today is sunny with a high of 75 degrees."

Virtual assistants can also be used for more complex tasks such as making reservations, setting reminders, and providing personalized recommendations. For example, a user might ask "What are some good Italian restaurants nearby?" The virtual assistant would use NLP to understand the user's request and generate a list of Italian restaurants in the user's vicinity.

Virtual assistants can be integrated into a wide range of devices, including smartphones, smart speakers, and smart home devices. They are becoming increasingly popular in various applications such as customer service, e-commerce, and healthcare.

As an AI prompt engineer, it's important to have a deep understanding of NLP techniques and AI technologies to develop effective virtual assistants. By using advanced AI algorithms such as deep learning and reinforcement learning, prompt engineers can develop virtual assistants that are more intelligent and personalized to the needs of users.

Sentiment Analysis: Sentiment analysis is the process of using NLP to determine the emotional tone of a piece of text, such as a tweet or a review. Sentiment analysis can be used to monitor public opinion about a brand, product, or service.

Example: A company using sentiment analysis to monitor social media to gauge public perception about their product.

Sentiment analysis, also known as opinion mining, is a natural language processing technique used to identify and extract subjective information from text data, such as opinions, emotions, and attitudes.

Sentiment analysis is used in a wide range of applications such as customer feedback analysis, social media monitoring, and brand reputation management. It can help businesses understand how customers feel about their products or services and identify areas for improvement.

There are various techniques used for sentiment analysis, including lexicon-based, machine learning-based, and hybrid approaches.

Lexicon-based approaches use sentiment dictionaries or lexicons to assign a sentiment score to each word in the text data. The sentiment score is typically a numerical value ranging from -1 to 1, with negative values indicating negative sentiment and positive values indicating positive sentiment. The sentiment score of each word is then aggregated to obtain an overall sentiment score for the entire text.

Machine learning-based approaches use algorithms such as decision trees, support vector machines, and neural networks to train models that can classify text data into positive, negative, or neutral sentiment categories. These approaches require labeled data for training and can achieve higher accuracy than lexicon-based approaches.

Hybrid approaches combine both lexicon-based and machine learning-based techniques to improve the accuracy of sentiment analysis.

Example: Let's consider an example of sentiment analysis on customer reviews of a restaurant.

Text Data: The restaurant collects customer reviews from various sources such as social media, online review sites, and feedback forms.

Sentiment Analysis: The restaurant uses sentiment analysis techniques to analyze the text data and extract the sentiment of each review.

Sentiment Score: Each review is assigned a sentiment score based on the sentiment analysis technique used. The sentiment score is a numerical value ranging from -1 to 1, with negative values indicating negative sentiment and positive values indicating positive sentiment.

Sentiment Category: The sentiment score of each review is then used to classify the review into a positive, negative, or neutral sentiment category. The restaurant can then use this information to identify areas for improvement and provide better customer service.

Sentiment analysis can also be used in social media monitoring to track public opinion about a particular topic or brand. For example, a company can use sentiment analysis to analyze tweets related to their brand and identify areas for improvement in their marketing strategy.

As a prompt engineer, it's important to have a deep understanding of NLP techniques and machine learning algorithms to develop effective sentiment analysis models. By using advanced algorithms such as deep learning and ensemble learning, prompt engineers can improve the accuracy of sentiment analysis and provide more valuable insights to businesses.

Text Classification

Text classification is the process of categorizing text into predefined categories using NLP techniques. Text classification can be used for various applications such as spam filtering, content recommendation, and topic modeling.

Example: A news website using text classification to recommend articles based on user preferences.

Text classification, also known as text categorization, is a natural language processing technique used to automatically classify text data into predefined categories.

Text classification is used in a wide range of applications such as spam filtering, sentiment analysis, and content categorization. It can help businesses automate the process of organizing large amounts of text data and improve the efficiency of various tasks such as customer service and content moderation.

There are various techniques used for text classification, including rule-based, statistical-based, and machine learning-based approaches.

Rule-based approaches use predefined rules or heuristics to classify text data into categories. These approaches are simple and easy to implement but may not be very accurate and require domain-specific knowledge.

Statistical-based approaches use algorithms such as Naive Bayes, decision trees, and logistic regression to learn patterns and relationships between text data and predefined categories from a labeled dataset. These approaches can achieve high accuracy but require large amounts of labeled data for training.

Machine learning-based approaches use deep learning algorithms such as Convolutional Neural Networks (CNNs) and Recurrent Neural Networks (RNNs) to learn complex representations of text data and classify it into categories. These approaches can achieve even higher accuracy and require less labeled data for training.

Example: Let's consider an example of text classification for spam filtering.

Text Data: An email service provider receives a large amount of email data, some of which are spam.

Text Preprocessing: The email data is preprocessed to remove stop words, punctuation, and special characters, and the remaining text is converted to numerical representations such as bag-of-words or word embeddings.

Text Classification: The email data is classified into spam or non-spam categories using a text classification model.

Model Training: A machine learning algorithm such as CNN or RNN is trained on a labeled dataset of email data to learn patterns and relationships between text data and predefined categories.

Model Evaluation: The trained model is evaluated on a separate dataset to test its accuracy and performance.

Model Deployment: The trained model is deployed to the email service provider's system to automatically classify incoming email data into spam or non-spam categories.

Text classification can also be used for content categorization, sentiment analysis, and topic modeling. For example, a news website can use text classification to categorize news articles into different topics such as sports, politics, and entertainment.

Text classification, also known as text categorization, is a natural language processing technique used to automatically classify text data into predefined categories.

Text classification is used in a wide range of applications such as spam filtering, sentiment analysis, and content categorization. It can help businesses automate the process of organizing large amounts of text data and improve the efficiency of various tasks such as customer service and content moderation.

There are various techniques used for text classification, including rule-based, statistical-based, and machine learning-based approaches.

Rule-based approaches use predefined rules or heuristics to classify text data into categories. These approaches are simple and easy to implement but may not be very accurate and require domain-specific knowledge.

Statistical-based approaches use algorithms such as Naive Bayes, decision trees, and logistic regression to learn patterns and relationships between text data and predefined categories from a labeled dataset. These approaches can achieve high accuracy but require large amounts of labeled data for training.

Machine learning-based approaches use deep learning algorithms such as Convolutional Neural Networks (CNNs) and Recurrent Neural Networks (RNNs) to learn complex representations of text data and classify it into categories. These approaches can achieve even higher accuracy and require less labeled data for training.

Example: Let's consider an example of text classification for spam filtering.

Text Data: An email service provider receives a large amount of email data, some of which are spam.

Text Preprocessing: The email data is preprocessed to remove stop words, punctuation, and special characters, and the remaining text is converted to numerical representations such as bag-of-words or word embeddings.

Text Classification: The email data is classified into spam or non-spam categories using a text classification model.

Model Training: A machine learning algorithm such as CNN or RNN is trained on a labeled dataset of email data to learn patterns and relationships between text data and predefined categories.

Model Evaluation: The trained model is evaluated on a separate dataset to test its accuracy and performance.

Model Deployment: The trained model is deployed to the email service provider's system to automatically classify incoming email data into spam or non-spam categories.

Text classification can also be used for content categorization, sentiment analysis, and topic modeling. For example, a news website can use text classification to categorize news articles into different topics such as sports, politics, and entertainment.

As a prompt engineer, it's important to have a deep understanding of NLP techniques and machine learning algorithms to develop effective text classification models. By using advanced algorithms such as deep learning and transfer learning, prompt engineers can improve the accuracy of text classification and provide more valuable insights to businesses.

As a prompt engineer, it's important to have a deep understanding of NLP techniques and machine learning algorithms to develop effective text classification models. By using advanced algorithms such as deep learning and transfer learning, prompt engineers can improve the accuracy of text classification and provide more valuable insights to businesses.

Machine Translation: Machine Translation is the process of automatically translating text from one language to another using NLP techniques. Machine Translation can be used to improve communication between people who speak different languages.

Example: Google Translate is a popular Machine Translation system that uses NLP to automatically translate text from one language to another.

Speech Recognition: Speech recognition is the process of using NLP to recognize spoken language and convert it into text or commands. Speech recognition can be used for various applications such as virtual assistants, automated customer service, and language learning.

Example: Amazon's Alexa is a virtual assistant that uses speech recognition to understand user queries and provide relevant responses.

NLP is used in many applications, from chatbots and virtual assistants to sentiment analysis and machine translation.

By using mathematical models such as neural networks and decision trees, prompt engineers can develop NLP systems that accurately understand natural language input and provide relevant responses or actions.

Future Directions and Opportunities for Research and Development

The field of NLP and prompt engineering is constantly evolving, and there are many exciting opportunities for research and development.

Some future directions and opportunities include:

Multilingual NLP

With the increasing global use of the internet, there is a growing need for multilingual NLP systems that can analyze and process text data in multiple languages. This presents an opportunity for prompt engineers to develop algorithms that can handle multilingual data and improve the accuracy of machine translation and cross-lingual text classification.

Multilingual NLP is the study of natural language processing (NLP) techniques that can analyze and process text data in multiple languages. With the increasing global use of the internet, there is a growing need for NLP systems that can handle multilingual data and improve the accuracy of machine translation and cross-lingual text classification.

One example of multilingual NLP is the use of parallel corpora

139

to train machine translation models. Parallel corpora are collections of texts in two or more languages that are aligned at the sentence or phrase level. By using parallel corpora, machine translation models can learn to translate between languages without the need for explicit bilingual dictionaries or manual annotation.

Another example of multilingual NLP is the use of cross-lingual embeddings, which are vector representations of words that capture their semantic and syntactic properties. By training cross-lingual embeddings on large amounts of multilingual data, NLP models can better handle multilingual text data and improve the accuracy of tasks such as cross-lingual text classification and named entity recognition.

Multilingual NLP has numerous applications in areas such as international business, social media analysis, and global health. For example, a company that operates in multiple countries may need to analyze customer feedback in different languages to identify common issues and areas for improvement. Similarly, public health organizations may need to monitor social media activity in multiple languages to track the spread of disease outbreaks.

As a prompt engineer, understanding the principles of multilingual NLP and how to apply them to real-world problems is an important skill. By leveraging techniques such as parallel corpora and cross-lingual embeddings, prompt engineers can develop more accurate and effective NLP models that can handle multilingual text data and improve the accuracy of machine translation and cross-lingual text classification.

Explainable NLP
As NLP models become more complex, there is a growing need for explainable NLP systems that can provide insights into how the model works and why it makes certain predictions. This presents an opportunity for prompt engineers to develop algorithms that can provide transparent and interpretable explanations for NLP models.

Explainable NLP (Natural Language Processing) is an approach to designing NLP models that can provide transparent and interpretable explanations for their decisions and predictions. As NLP models become more complex, there is a growing need for explainable NLP systems that can provide insights into how the model works and why it makes certain predictions. This is particularly important in applications such as healthcare, finance, and law where the decisions made by NLP models can have significant consequences.

One example of explainable NLP is the use of attention mechanisms to visualize which parts of the input text are most important for making a particular prediction. Attention mechanisms allow NLP models to focus on certain parts of the input text while ignoring others, and can provide insights into how the model is making its decision. For example, in a sentiment analysis task, attention mechanisms can be used to highlight the words or phrases in the input text that are most strongly associated with positive or negative sentiment.

Another example of explainable NLP is the use of rule-based systems to provide explicit and interpretable decision-making rules for NLP models. Rule-based systems use human-defined rules to make decisions, which can be more easily understood and explained than the black-box decision-making processes of traditional machine learning models. Rule-based systems can also be combined with machine learning techniques to provide a hybrid approach that balances the accuracy of machine learning with the transparency and interpretability of rule-based systems.

Explainable NLP has numerous applications in areas such as healthcare, legal analysis, and financial decision-making. For example, in healthcare, explainable NLP can be used to provide transparent and interpretable explanations for medical diagnoses and treatment recommendations. Similarly, in finance, explainable

NLP can be used to provide insights into the factors that influence investment decisions and risk assessments.

As a prompt engineer, understanding the principles of explainable NLP and how to apply them to real-world problems is an important skill. By leveraging techniques such as attention mechanisms and rule-based systems, prompt engineers can develop more transparent and interpretable NLP models that can provide valuable insights to businesses and organizations.

Personalized NLP

With the increasing amount of data generated by individuals, there is a growing need for personalized NLP systems that can analyze and process text data based on individual preferences and behavior. This presents an opportunity for prompt engineers to develop algorithms that can personalize NLP models and improve the accuracy of personalized recommendations and search results.

Personalized NLP (Natural Language Processing) is a branch of NLP that focuses on tailoring NLP models to individual users based on their preferences, behaviors, and characteristics. Personalized NLP systems can provide more accurate and relevant recommendations, predictions, and responses by taking into account each user's unique context and history.

One example of personalized NLP is personalized recommendation systems that use user history and behavior to provide more relevant recommendations for products or services. For example, a personalized movie recommendation system can use a user's viewing history, ratings, and other information to recommend movies that are likely to be of interest to that particular user.

Another example of personalized NLP is personalized chatbots that use natural language processing techniques to understand user input and provide personalized responses. Personalized chatbots can be trained on specific user data such as conversation history, user preferences, and behavioral patterns to provide more accurate and relevant responses.

Personalized NLP has numerous applications in areas such as e-commerce, healthcare, and customer service. For example, in e-commerce, personalized NLP can be used to provide customized product recommendations and improve the overall shopping experience. In healthcare, personalized NLP can be used to provide more accurate and tailored medical diagnoses and treatment recommendations.

As a prompt engineer, understanding the principles of personalized NLP and how to apply them to real-world problems is an important skill. By leveraging techniques such as recommendation systems and chatbots that are personalized to individual users, prompt engineers can develop more accurate and effective NLP models that provide personalized experiences to users.

Domain-Specific NLP

There is a growing need for domain-specific NLP systems that can analyze and process text data in specialized fields such as medicine, finance, and law.

This presents an opportunity for prompt engineers to develop algorithms that can handle domain-specific terminology and improve the accuracy of text classification and information extraction in specialized domains.

Domain-specific NLP (Natural Language Processing) is a type of NLP that is tailored to specific domains or subject areas, such as healthcare, finance, or legal.

Domain-specific NLP models are trained on specific language and vocabulary associated with the domain, and are designed to understand and generate text that is specific to that domain.

One example of domain-specific NLP is medical NLP, which is used in the healthcare industry to improve the accuracy and efficiency of medical diagnoses, treatment recommendations, and other medical tasks.

Medical NLP models are trained on medical terminologies, vocabulary, and language patterns, and can recognize medical concepts and entities such as diseases, symptoms, medications, and procedures.

Another example of domain-specific NLP is financial NLP, which is used in the finance industry to analyze financial data, detect fraud, and provide insights into investment decisions.

Financial NLP models are trained on financial language and jargon, and can recognize financial concepts and entities such as stock tickers, financial ratios, and market trends.

Domain-specific NLP has numerous applications in various industries and domains, including legal, customer service, and e-commerce.

For example, legal NLP can be used to analyze legal documents, extract relevant information, and provide legal advice. Customer service NLP can be used to improve the quality and efficiency of customer support interactions, by understanding customer inquiries and providing relevant information.

As a prompt engineer, understanding the principles of domain-specific NLP and how to apply them to real-world problems is an important skill.

By developing domain-specific NLP models that are tailored to specific domains and subject areas, prompt engineers can improve the accuracy and efficiency of NLP systems, and provide better insights and recommendations to businesses and organizations operating in these domains.

NLP for Low-Resource Languages

There is a growing need for NLP systems that can analyze and process text data in low-resource languages that have limited amounts of labeled data.

This presents an opportunity for prompt engineers to develop algorithms that can leverage transfer learning and unsupervised learning to improve the accuracy of NLP models in low-resource languages.

Examples of ongoing research and development in these areas include the development of explainable AI models such as LIME and SHAP, the use of transfer learning and pre-trained language models such as BERT and GPT-3 for multilingual NLP, and the development of personalized recommender systems based on user behavior and preferences.

NLP (Natural Language Processing) for low-resource languages refers to the development of NLP systems for languages with limited linguistic resources, such as small corpora, few annotated data, and low-quality speech recognition and machine translation models.

Developing NLP systems for low-resource languages is important for improving communication and access to information in these communities.

One example of NLP for low-resource languages is the development of speech recognition models for indigenous languages. These languages often have limited speech resources, making it challenging to develop accurate and efficient speech recognition systems. However, by leveraging techniques such as data augmentation and transfer learning, NLP researchers have been able to develop speech recognition models for low-resource languages that achieve competitive performance.

Another example of NLP for low-resource languages is the development of machine translation models. Low-resource languages often have limited parallel corpora, making it challenging to develop high-quality machine translation models. However, by using techniques such as unsupervised and semi-supervised learning, researchers have been able to develop machine translation models for low-resource languages that achieve reasonable translation quality.

NLP for low-resource languages has numerous applications in various domains, such as education, healthcare, and government.

For example, NLP systems can be used to translate medical information and documents to low-resource languages, improving access to healthcare for individuals in these communities.

NLP systems can also be used to develop educational materials in low-resource languages, providing greater access to education for individuals in these communities.

As a prompt engineer, understanding the challenges and opportunities of NLP for low-resource languages is an important skill.

By leveraging techniques such as transfer learning and unsupervised learning, prompt engineers can develop NLP systems that are effective and efficient, even for languages with limited linguistic resources.

This can improve communication and access to information in these communities, providing greater opportunities for individuals and businesses operating in low-resource language environments.

As a prompt engineer, it's important to stay up-to-date with the latest research and development in the field of NLP and identify new opportunities for innovation and improvement.

By staying current with the latest advancements in machine learning and NLP, prompt engineers can develop more accurate and effective NLP models that can provide valuable insights to businesses and organizations.

CONCLUSION

The field of NLP prompt engineering has made significant strides in recent years, thanks to the use of advanced mathematics and machine learning techniques.

By leveraging techniques such as probability theory, linear algebra, calculus, optimization, and others, prompt engineers can develop NLP systems that are accurate, efficient, and scalable.

This book has covered a wide range of topics, including the foundations of mathematics for NLP, NLP modeling techniques, advanced mathematics for NLP, designing effective prompts using mathematics, evaluating prompt quality using metrics such as perplexity and BLEU score, and applications of NLP prompt engineering in various domains.

We have discussed examples of NLP applications, such as machine translation, sentiment analysis, text summarization, and question-answering. We have also explored the use of NLP in chatbots, virtual assistants, and other NLP systems.

The book has emphasized the importance of domain-specific NLP, multilingual NLP, explainable NLP, and personalized NLP.

We have discussed the challenges and opportunities of NLP for low-resource languages, as well as the future directions and opportunities for research and development in NLP prompt engineering.

By understanding the principles and techniques of NLP prompt engineering, and by applying them to real-world problems, prompt engineers can help businesses and organizations to improve their NLP systems, and to provide better insights and recommendations to their customers and clients.

We hope this book has provided a comprehensive overview of NLP prompt engineering and mathematics and has inspired readers to explore the many opportunities and possibilities of this exciting field.

Summary of key Takeaways and Insights

As a prompt engineer, it's important to understand some of the key takeaways and insights from the book to apply them effectively in NLP systems. Here are some of the most important takeaways and insights:

Mathematics is the foundation of NLP prompt engineering. Probability theory, linear algebra, calculus, and optimization are essential mathematical tools that prompt engineers must understand to develop effective NLP systems.

NLP modeling techniques such as bag-of-words, word embeddings, neural networks, probabilistic models, and graph-based models are powerful tools for NLP prompt engineering.

The use of advanced mathematics such as singular value decomposition, tf-idf, and entropy can significantly improve the accuracy and efficiency of NLP systems.

Evaluating prompt quality using metrics such as perplexity and BLEU score is essential to developing effective NLP systems.

Domain-specific NLP, multilingual NLP, explainable NLP, and personalized NLP are all critical areas for NLP prompt engineering, as they allow prompt engineers to develop systems that are tailored to specific contexts and user needs.

NLP applications such as machine translation, sentiment analysis, text summarization, and question-answering have numerous applications in various domains, such as education, healthcare, and government.

Developing NLP systems for low-resource languages is challenging, but leveraging techniques such as unsupervised and semi-supervised learning can improve the quality of NLP systems for these languages.

By understanding these key takeaways and insights, prompt engineers can develop NLP systems that are accurate, efficient, and effective in solving real-world problems.

Final Thoughts on the Role of Mathematics in NLP Prompt Engineering

The role of mathematics in NLP prompt engineering cannot be overstated. Mathematics provides a foundation for understanding the complex statistical models and algorithms that power NLP systems, allowing prompt engineers to design and develop systems that are accurate, efficient, and scalable.

Through the use of mathematical techniques such as probability theory, linear algebra, calculus, optimization, and graph theory, prompt engineers can model and analyze natural language data to extract meaning, identify patterns and relationships, and generate effective prompts.

For example, the bag-of-words model, which is a common NLP modeling technique, uses linear algebra to represent text documents as vectors of word frequencies.

This allows prompt engineers to perform operations such as document similarity, clustering, and classification, which are useful in many NLP applications.

Similarly, techniques such as neural networks and probabilistic models leverage calculus and probability theory to create powerful and effective NLP systems, capable of complex tasks such as language generation, machine translation, and text classification.

Furthermore, the use of optimization algorithms such as gradient descent, genetic algorithms, and simulated annealing can help prompt engineers to fine-tune and optimize NLP models, improving their accuracy and efficiency.

Overall, mathematics plays a crucial role in NLP prompt engineering, enabling prompt engineers to develop sophisticated and effective NLP systems.

By leveraging the principles and techniques of mathematics, prompt engineers can continue to push the boundaries of what's possible in the field of NLP, creating innovative solutions to complex natural language problems.

APPENDIX A:
GLOSSARY

A* Search - A search algorithm used to find the shortest path between two points in a graph or network.

Bag-of-Words Model - A text representation model that ignores the order of words in a document and counts their frequency.

Beam Search - A search algorithm used in natural language processing to generate likely sequences of words given a particular input.

BLEU score - A metric used to evaluate the quality of machine-translated text by comparing it to a human-generated reference translation.

Calculus - The branch of mathematics that deals with continuous change and motion.

Chatbots - Computer programs designed to simulate conversation with human users.

Conditional Probability Table - A table used in Bayesian Networks to represent the probability of an event given its parents' states.

Conditional Random Fields - A probabilistic model used for structured prediction tasks, such as sequence labeling or image segmentation.

Decision Tree - A predictive modeling tool used to map observations about an item to a conclusion about its target value. A tree-like model used to make decisions based on input variables.

Deep Belief Networks - A type of neural network architecture used for unsupervised learning and generative modeling.

Document Classification - The task of assigning a label or category to a document based on its content or features.
Domain-Specific NLP - NLP systems designed to perform specific tasks within a particular domain.

Entropy - A measure of the uncertainty associated with a random variable, often used in information theory to quantify the amount of information contained in a message or dataset.

Explainable NLP - NLP systems that provide transparent and understandable outputs and reasoning.

Feedforward Neural Network - A neural network architecture where information flows in only one direction, from input to output.

Genetic Algorithms - A metaheuristic optimization technique inspired by the process of natural selection, used to find the best solution to a problem.

Gradient Descent - An optimization algorithm used to minimize a function by iteratively adjusting the parameters.

Graph Theory - The branch of mathematics that deals with the study of graphs and their properties.

Graph-Based Models - NLP models that leverage graph structures to represent and analyze natural language data.

Information Theory - The mathematical study of communication, focusing on the quantification of information and the transmission of data.

Knowledge Graphs - A knowledge representation technique used to model concepts, entities, and their relationships.

Latent Dirichlet Allocation - A statistical model used to discover topics in a corpus of text documents.

Linear Algebra - The branch of mathematics that deals with vector spaces and linear mappings between them.

Long Short-Term Memory Networks - A type of recurrent neural network architecture capable of learning long-term dependencies in sequential data.

Low-Resource Languages - Languages with limited data and resources for NLP systems to work with.

Machine Translation - The process of automatically translating text from one language to another, often using NLP models and techniques.

Markov Models - A statistical modeling approach used to represent sequential data, where the probability of a particular event is dependent only on the preceding event.

Markov Random Fields - A probabilistic graphical model used to represent complex joint distributions over random variables.

Multilingual NLP - NLP systems that can understand and process multiple languages.

Multi-Task Learning - A machine learning technique where a single model is trained to perform multiple related tasks simultaneously, often leading to improved performance on all tasks.

Named Entity Disambiguation - The process of identifying the correct entity for a given named entity mention in a text.

Named Entity Linking - The process of linking named entities to their corresponding knowledge base entries.

Named Entity Recognition - The process of identifying and extracting named entities such as names, places, and organizations from text.

Natural Language Generation - The process of generating text or speech in a natural language, often used in chatbots or virtual assistants.

Neural Networks - Artificial intelligence systems that are inspired by the structure and function of the human brain.

NLP - Natural Language Processing

Optimization - The process of finding the best solution to a problem.

Particle Swarm Optimization - A metaheuristic optimization algorithm that simulates the behavior of a swarm of particles moving towards a common goal.

Perplexity - A statistical measure used to evaluate the effectiveness of language models in predicting the next word in a sequence.

Personalized NLP - NLP systems that can tailor outputs and experiences to individual users.

Probabilistic Context-Free Grammars - A probabilistic grammar used to generate sentences and parse natural language sentences. A family of probabilistic models used for modeling complex systems with multiple interacting variables.

Probability Theory - The branch of mathematics that deals with the analysis of random phenomena.

Prompt Engineering - The process of designing and developing prompts for NLP systems.

Question Answering - The task of generating an answer to a question posed in natural language.

Recurrent Neural Networks - A type of neural network architecture commonly used in NLP that is capable of processing sequences of variable length.

Sentiment Analysis - A natural language processing task that involves identifying and extracting subjective information from text, including opinions, attitudes, and emotions.

Sentiment Classification - The task of determining the sentiment expressed in a piece of text as positive, negative, or neutral.

Simulated Annealing - A global optimization algorithm that simulates the physical process of annealing to find the global minimum of a function.

Singular Value Decomposition - A mathematical technique used to decompose a matrix into its constituent parts, often used in text analysis for dimensionality reduction.

Speech Recognition - The process of converting spoken language into text.

Text Clustering - The process of grouping similar documents or pieces of text into clusters based on their content or characteristics.

Text Summarization - The process of creating a shorter, condensed version of a text document while retaining its most important information.

Text-to-Speech - The process of converting written text into spoken language using natural language processing techniques.

TF-IDF - A technique used in text analysis to quantify the importance of a word in a document.

Topic Modeling - A statistical model used to extract topics from a collection of documents.

Transformer Model - A neural network architecture used for natural language processing tasks, including language generation and translation.

Virtual Assistants - AI-powered systems that can assist with tasks and answer questions in natural language.

Word Embeddings - A language modeling technique that maps words to vectors in a high-dimensional space, capturing semantic relationships between them.

Word Sense Disambiguation - The process of determining the correct meaning of a word in context.